Praise for Speak

It is a special voice that can lead the next generation of believers from within. One who understands every struggle and disappointment, one who has walked away and come back, one who is both prophetic and compassionate. Nish Weiseth is unquestionably one of those leaders. *Speak* is just impossibly hopeful. It tells of a better way, better community, better grace, better story. You nod, you cry, you shout, and ultimately you go quiet and whisper, "Lord, here is my life; may it speak of You."

> JEN HATMAKER, author of *Interrupted* and
> *7: An Experimental Mutiny Against Excess*

Speak is a powerful, honest, bridge-building book that is at once inspiring and practical, brave and wise. With the skill of a master storyteller and the presence of a friend, Nish Weiseth guides us through the holy ground of one another's stories and invites us to take off our shoes. This is a must-read for anyone who longs to move beyond the division, vitriol, and platitudes that characterize so much of modern dialogue and instead engage in the joy and hard work of loving one another well.

> RACHEL HELD EVANS, author of *Faith Unraveled* and
> the *New York Times* bestseller *A Year of Biblical Womanhood*

Speak is a much-needed antidote to the evangelical hero complex. If you've ever felt like your story isn't enough — not cool enough, not interesting enough, not fascinating enough, not doing enough — you need to read this book. Your story matters — in fact, it just might change the world.

> SARAH BESSEY, author of *Jesus Feminist*

The trouble with *Speak* is that I couldn't decide whether to keep reading or *go tell my story to anyone who would listen*. I did both. I read *Speak* all the way through, and then I immediately sat down to write my heart out. This book will inspire you to *get on with it already*. Nish gives us permission to believe we are worthy of the space we occupy, courage to accept that our struggles and stories matter, and hope that all we must to do to free ourselves and others is to SPEAK our hearts.

GLENNON DOYLE MELTON, *New York Times* bestselling author of *Carry On, Warrior: The Power of Embracing Your Messy, Beautiful Life* and founder of Momastery.com

Speak is a sane and needed call for a new kind of dialogue—one that leans on the human story as a place for finding common ground. Nish pushes us to consider the value of vulnerability and the power of the personal in our everyday interactions and our most impassioned debates, making the case that our story can be the key to bridge building and understanding. The book weaves in compelling stories of other writers whose own stories have changed the dialogue on many difficult issues. Full of nuance and wisdom, *Speak* sets the stage for a better way of relating to others.

KRISTEN HOWERTON, author of *Rage Against the Minivan*

Speak is a remarkably well-crafted exploration of how individual and communal experiences together shape and inform the kingdom of God. Nish Weiseth's strong and compelling prose both tasks and equips readers to be bestowers of grace and receivers of one another's stories. Convicting, authentic, and profoundly kind—this is a must-read.

PRESTON YANCEY, author of *Tables in the Wilderness: A Memoir of God Found, Lost, and Found Again*

Speak boldly calls readers to share their stories of conversion in our clashing, ever-debating culture. From personal experience of sharing my biggest fear, I wholeheartedly recommend reading Speak to experience the freedom of storytelling.

REBEKAH LYONS, author of *Freefall to Fly*

In a world that so often chooses to see people as statistics, Nish Weiseth challenges us to see something better: stories. In these pages, she offers a way past that which is alienating and divisive and leads into the heart of relationship.

ADDIE ZIERMAN, author of *When We Were on Fire: A Memoir of Consuming Faith, Tangled Love, and Starting Over*

Speak is a book about the humble power of storytelling, and Nish Weiseth spares none of us — each story a softening blow to stony hearts, a gathering of confidence, a sense of shared experience, a realization of how interwoven I am into a transformative narrative. Nish brings out the simple and the honest. If you need to get rid of the fear of revealing your true self, read *Speak* and evoke within yourself a great love for others right where they are.

AMBER C. HAINES, writer at TheRunaMuck.com and upcoming author with Revell

Speak invites readers to reconnect with the time-honored tradition of truth-telling through story. By telling stories we find that the truth is deeper, wider, and far more complex than we could ever imagine, but we'll also discover the raw materials we need to change the world. If you're weary of sermons with three-point outlines and tidy application points, this book will direct you to the liberating craft of storytelling.

ED CYZEWSKI, author of *A Christian Survival Guide: A Lifeline to Faith and Growth and Coffeehouse Theology*

What Nish has done here is remarkable. This is not just a book you read; it is a book you feel and a book that changes how you live. I will tell more stories because of it. I know you will too. Bravo.

ANNIE F. DOWNS, author of *Let's All Be Brave*

Nish Weiseth is a gifted storyteller, but the paramount gift of *Speak* is her invitation to tell our own stories: around the hearth, over cups of coffee, and along the path as we walk together in the ways of Jesus. I'm newly convinced that sharing our lives will truly change our lives — and the world.

KATHERINE WILLIS PERSHEY, author of *Any Day a Beautiful Change*

Nish Weiseth is a grand storyteller, a kind whose prose makes you feel like you've known her your entire life. In *Speak*, Weiseth uses that gift of narrative to remind us of the power and importance of telling our stories, engaging other people's stories, and embracing life and faith through the affecting lens of narrative, myth, and truth. Full of wisdom, passion, and insight, *Speak* is one of those books you'll return to for renewal again and again.

MATTHEW PAUL TURNER, author of *Churched* and *Our Great Big American God*

Heartfelt, honest, and full of grace, *Speak* unpacks the transformative power of sharing our experiences rather than our opinions. Nish Weiseth beautifully reminds us that while rhetoric often creates division and builds walls, vulnerability opens the door to true relationship.

ALECE RONZINO, founder of OneWord365 and blogger at GritAndGlory.com

Jun-28-2014

94359_CRC_1403

speak

speak

HOW YOUR STORY CAN **CHANGE** THE WORLD

Nish Weiseth

ZONDERVAN®

ZONDERVAN

Speak
Copyright © 2014 by Nish Weiseth

This title is also available as a Zondervan ebook.
Visit www.zondervan.com/ebooks.

Requests for information should be addressed to:

Zondervan, 3900 *Sparks Dr. SE, Grand Rapids, Michigan 49546*

Library of Congress Cataloging-in-Publication Data

Weiseth, Nish, 1983–
    Speak : how your story can change the world / Nish Weiseth. —
1st [edition].
        pages cm
    ISBN 978-0-310-33817-8 (softcover)
      1. Storytelling—Religious aspects—Christianity. 2. Witness bearing
(Christianity) 3. Postmodernism—Religious aspects—Christianity.
I. Title.
    BT83.78.W45   2014
    248'.5—dc23   2014008436

All Scripture quotations, unless otherwise indicated, are taken from The
Holy Bible, *New International Version®, NIV®.* Copyright © 1973, 1978, 1984,
2011 by Biblica, Inc.® Used by permission. All rights reserved worldwide.

Scripture quotations marked MSG are taken from *The Message.* Copyright
© 1993, 1994, 1995, 1996, 2000, 2001, 2002. Used by permission of NavPress
Publishing Group.

Any Internet addresses (websites, blogs, etc.) and telephone numbers in
this book are offered as a resource. They are not intended in any way to be
or imply an endorsement by Zondervan, nor does Zondervan vouch for the
content of these sites and numbers for the life of this book.

Published in association with literary agent Jenni Burke of D.C. Jacobson &
Associates LLC, an Author Management Company. www.dcjacobson.com

Cover design: Jamie DeBruyn
Cover and interior image: iStockphoto LP; © vasabii / iStockphoto LP
Interior design: Beth Shagene

First Printing June 2014 / Printed in the United States of America

For Erik.
The greatest chapter of my story.

Contents

The Outcome:
Story Changes the World

Foreword by Shauna Niequist

I'm a story girl—I always have been. Apologetics and debate make me cranky. I glaze over at numbers and statistics. But tell me a story and I'm hooked. Tell me a story and I'll never forget it. Tell me a story and I'll carry it with me wherever I go, like a penny in a pocket, like a friend.

The conversation our culture is having right now can hardly be called a conversation—so pitched, so loud, so obsessed with being heard and not at all concerned with hearing. We label and stereotype; we identify who's in and who's out; we define ourselves by who we vote for and what cars we drive and what zip codes we live in. And we define other people by who they vote for, what they drive, and what zip codes they live in.

Our culture specializes in boxes, in categories, in labels. We think we know everything there is to know about someone because they send their kids to this or that kind of school, or because they go this or that kind of church, or because they have this or that kind of sticker on their car. This is sloppy. And this is dangerous.

And this is why story matters. Because when you listen to a story, you have to give up your stereotypes and your labels. Because stories crawl out of the boxes every chance they get. Because stories zig when we think they'll zag. Stories surprise us around every corner. Stories reach out and grab our labels and shred them to confetti.

There was a person in my life who made me crazy. She made me mad and made me nervous. She was control, control, control. Perfection, perfection, perfection. Her anxiety brought out my anxiety, and being around her exhausted me. So I did what we do with people who make us crazy. I labeled her: *control freak*. I congratulated myself for being laid-back, especially compared to Little Miss Hand-Sanitizer-on-Everything.

And then one night, when we were up so late we stopped editing our words and let them all fall out in a jumble, she told me about what life was like for her as a little girl. She told me about how, when she was still in elementary school, she practically lived at the hospital when her mom was dying, and how careful they had to be about germs. Her little girl-self took it upon herself to never, never, never be dirty because it could make her mom sick.

There it is, I realized. I blushed with shame, furious with myself that I had done it again: I labeled and distanced. I didn't listen. And when I finally did listen, the story I heard made it all make sense—the control, the perfectionism, that crazy hand sanitizer all the time.

And aren't we all like that? Impossible. Crazy-making. Cartoons. Walking stereotypes. Until someone sticks around long enough to hear the story of how we got here, what winding journey brought us along, what diagnosis and hospital room and fear made us who we are.

A wise friend of mine is teaching me to ask this question every time I disagree with someone, and especially when I disagree in a visceral way: "How did that person come to feel this way?" Essentially, he's teaching me to ask, "What part of this person's story do I need to know to understand what he or she is telling me right now?"

Wouldn't that change everything?

When we listen, we're forced to drop our labels. When we listen to stories, there's no longer any room for stereotypes. We've had all the screaming and all the polarizing and all the labeling this world can handle. The only way into a better future is an entirely new way.

And that way is the way of story-telling, and story-listening. That way is about the details, the how-we-got-there, the way the sky looked when she said that thing that changed everything.

The way is story.

Because we've run the cartoon-and-label way into the ground. The cable news shouting matches are a dead end.

The new way through is story-telling and story-listening. It's unfamiliar at first, and scary, but over time, you find you begin to develop muscle memory for it. You find you begin to feel something like a holy curiosity for everyone you see: What's her story? How did he come to feel this way? What is it that I don't yet know about her story?

This is an exciting way to live. This is, I believe, a Kingdom way to live, because instead of straw men and cartoons, we begin to dwell in actual humanity, which was the plan all along, of course. Story draws us together, hands and voices and memories. It bridges the distances we've created, because we thought the distance would keep us safe. It doesn't. It only keeps us lonely.

My friend Nish knows all about this holy curiosity. She knows all about this Kingdom way of living. She knows, deep in her bones, that stories change us in ways that debates and statistics never will.

Nish is a story girl too, a kindred spirit, a sister. And honestly, I can't think of a better guide along this path ...

Introduction

The language of logical argument, of proofs, is the language of the limited self we know and can manipulate. But the language of parable and poetry, of storytelling, moves from the imprisoned language of the provable into the freed language of what I must, for lack of another word, continue to call faith.

MADELEINE L'ENGLE, *A CIRCLE OF QUIET*

I am a part of the millennial generation. We are in our twenties and thirties. Some of us are single, and some are married. Some of us have kids. Some don't. We are, as a group, overeducated and underemployed. Some of us are children of parents who were part of the Christian Coalition of the Reagan years. Some of us are children of parents who preferred the principles of the People for the American Way. We've got lots of tech savvy, but we're spiritually running on empty, and we're searching.

We're searching for God. We're searching for real, honest community. We're searching for significance and affirmation that, yes, our voices matter.

Our stories matter.

I am part of a generation on the brink of exploding in frustration. We're fed up. We're leaving the church. We've been injured, and we're growing more cynical by the day. We're tired of the heated, bloated rhetoric of those on opposite sides of political and theological divides. We're tired of oversimplified answers to nuanced questions, and we're tired of being apathetic.

I'm tired of being tired.

And that's why I'm writing this book.

I'm a blogger who writes primarily about my life, my experiences, and my opinions. On one hand, it's fantastic. It provides me with an immediate audience, immediate feedback, and, often, immediate praise.

Yet, on the other hand, there's also criticism, of course. Which I'm not averse to. I welcome it, particularly if it's constructive and offered with care. I believe "iron sharpens iron"—and I'm willing to be sharpened. However, the criticism I encounter as I write on the Internet can be harsh, personal, and unrelenting. Somehow the Internet gives people the idea they have carte blanche to treat others cruelly.

Have you ever read the comments section after an article on any of the news network websites? They are *rough*. In fact, I tell writers who haven't checked out the comments sections on news websites to never do so. When certain readers engage content on the web they disagree with, they seem to be emboldened by that anonymity to speak their minds. Why? Because they can. Unfiltered, unchecked, and with abandon.

When typing words onto a screen rather than talking with someone across a coffee-shop table, it becomes quite a bit harder to separate the person who wrote the content from the content itself. We forget that content is written by real people with real feelings, real experiences, and real lives. We forget that bloggers and writers on the Internet are actual people. And perhaps everyone hides behind some sort of anonymity on the web.

Here's an example: My friend Rachel wrote a piece for CNN Belief Blog about why the millennial generation is leaving the church in droves.[1] She had written about this phenomenon on her own blog previously, and she'd even admitted to painting a picture using generalities that don't apply to every single individual. She had simply identified what might be motivating twenty- and thirtysomethings to walk away from the church. It was a well-written piece that received over nine thousand comments on the CNN site.

Unfortunately, many of those comments were hurtful, personal, and vitriolic. One person wrote:

> I feel bad for this author. She mocks the idea of getting hipper bands or a coffee shop to bring people into the church, and writes: "Many of us, myself included, are finding ourselves increasingly drawn to high church traditions—Catholicism, Eastern Orthodoxy, the Episcopal Church, etc.— precisely because the ancient forms of liturgy seem so unpretentious, so unconcerned with being 'cool,' and we find that refreshingly authentic."
>
> Ah yes. Authentic bull. So so much better than that new-age edgy bull. Pumpkin, it's the same old bull just sold to you in a different package. Grow up. God is about as real as Hera and Zeus and Jupiter.[2]

Ouch.

That kind of hatred and intolerance on the Internet belongs to a breed all its own. The harsh rhetoric can rival that of some of the most outspoken, negative radio talk-show hosts. And you know where it can be the worst? On *Christian* websites and blogs!

Thoughtful, intelligent, Jesus-following Christians are declared unbiblical and un-Christlike when they choose to be brave and write about a tough subject. They're accused of mocking Scripture and not holding it in high enough regard. They're called *heretics*. I've seen them picked apart, chewed up, and spit out by other Christians, all in the name of Jesus. It's heartbreaking.

As a blogger, I'd become accustomed to watching these attacks unfold, and for a long time it kept me from writing bravely. I didn't want to be called out. I watched as my friends, who also *wanted* to address hard topics, wrote out of fear instead of bravery.

And yet some of the people I admire are able to courageously communicate their ideas effectively—like my dear friend and fellow author, Sarah Bessey. In her book *Jesus Feminist*, she tackles the sometimes-volatile issue of the equality and value of women in the kingdom of God, delicately weaving in her own stories and her experiences of being a woman in the church.

Another brave writer is Lauren Winner. In *Mudhouse Sabbath*, she discusses the rich practices of Orthodox Judaism—traditions she grew up with—and how they enrich her life as a practicing Christian. Remarkably, evangelical readers who would bristle at the thought of incorporating Jewish practices into their modern Christian faith walk began nodding their heads in agreement, drawn in by Winner's unique knack for telling stories from her own life. The gift from both Sarah Bessey and Lauren Winner is that they engage hot-button "issues" at a basic human level.

And they do it with story.

A Deeper Story

In the fall of 2010, I was blessed with the opportunity to meet and hear Ann Voskamp, author of the *New York Times* bestseller *One Thousand Gifts*. In her message, Ann made one remark that got under my skin. She was speaking about using writing as a way to glorify God when she instructed the audience, "Give me your story, not your sermon."

It was my "lightbulb" moment.

What if there was a place where writers could address all the hot topics and heavy issues without fear? What if there was a place where readers could engage *stories* rather than tired old rhetoric? What if, as Ann suggested, we started sharing our *stories* instead of our sermons? What would that look like?

Out of those questions, I took a leap of faith and created an online space called *A Deeper Story*, inviting some talented storytellers to join me. Our aim was simple: we would use the art of story and personal narrative to address some of the most troublesome topics found on the collision course between Christianity and culture.

For example, Addie Zierman wrote a brilliant piece about Christians using curse words, titled "In Defense of the 4-Letter Word."[3] Ashleigh Baker wrote a post that went viral, called "What I Won't Tell You about My Ballet Dancing Son."[4] In the post, she carefully navigates some of the cultural norms surrounding gender and children, emphasizing how proud she is of her son and his dancing abilities.

The best thing about *A Deeper Story* has been the overwhelming response from tens of thousands of monthly readers. The conversations, in the comments and through emails, have been uplifting and productive. In fact, the stories shared are propelling people to action. To my delight, readers are beginning to understand that we interact over issues best when there's a human connection.

At *A Deeper Story* writers are changing the game. Personal stories are changing hearts, building bridges, advocating for good, making disciples, and proclaiming God's kingdom breaking in on earth today.

This book is a call to do just that—to change the game by telling the stories of our lives with courage, honesty, and integrity. It's a call to acknowledge that each of our stories is a small piece of the greatest story —God's continual work and transforming power in our lives. It's also an invitation to approach the world's problems with renewed vision and passion. It's a call to engage with others based on what we have in common rather than on what divides us.

The stories of how God transforms our lives and of how we connect with other human beings can have incredible power and influence in our culture. For instance, my friend—and a writer for *A Deeper Story* —Erika Morrison, wrote a piece about how her family has begun to practice an original initiative they call "Plus One" (see her post about this at the end of chapter 6). Every week they adopt into their family a different person in need. That person becomes their "Plus One." If they go out for frozen yogurt, they invite someone to join them. If they're going to the grocery store, they buy an extra bag of groceries and seek out someone who needs it.

Since Erika wrote about the "Plus One" principle, I've gotten emails and comments from readers who have implemented this idea into their own families, working to help those in need and speaking value and love to those in their own communities who have lost hope. Because Erika was willing to write the story of her family's choices, several other families around the country are making a difference in the lives of people in their neighborhoods. It's the most beautiful kind of influence someone can have and hold.

Stories like Erika's can change the world.

Throughout the course of this book, you will get the chance to read some of the incredibly compelling stories that have been published at *A Deeper Story*. You'll see them at the end of every chapter—eight in total. The stories we picked are what I believe to be good examples of how personal narrative and story can be used to change lives, build bridges, affect change, and proclaim God's kingdom, and each story fits the theme for each chapter.

At the end of each of these eight stories, you'll get to see the responses of real people. The comments and conversations provided alongside each story are a small window into how the story of one person deeply affects the life of another. By simply having the courage to tell their stories, the writers of each piece significantly impacted the life of another person. It's my hope and prayer that as you read this book and the stories shared at the end of each chapter, you will be encouraged and motivated to tell your own story in unique, creative, and compelling ways—whether it's by starting a blog online or having coffee with a friend at a local coffee shop. There's no wrong way to share your story. The important thing, which you'll learn in the pages of this book, is that you have the courage to do it at all.

What Is Story?

Story has become a common buzzword in evangelical circles. Conferences, books, magazines, and blogs talk about the use of story and the importance of personal narrative to propel the forward motion of the gospel. But what does *story* really mean?

Here, *story* is the vulnerable sharing of your life experiences with others. It includes everything from the relationships you have with others today to the awkward moments in high school that you can't erase from your memory, no matter how hard you try. Your story includes how and where you grew up and the impact they both had on your life. It also refers to the mistakes you've made along the way. Sharing your story allows others to glimpse how you've been shaped, what matters to you, and why it matters.

The power of story becomes evident when, as we share, another's eyes light up and they say, "You too? Me too!" The walls of isolation we build around ourselves, believing we are the only ones who feel a certain way, come tumbling down when we're vulnerable and honest with each other about both our struggles and our victories. When I am brave enough to share my story, I'm actually reaching out to you, allowing you to cross over whatever divide is between us. By vulnerably offering you my hand, I'm building a bridge between us through my story.

One of the most significant parts of our stories feels very vulnerable and personal, and that is *our relationship with God*. So often, we minimize our story when we tell only our conversion experience. Certainly your conversion is a part of your story, but there's so much more. Your story includes your life before encountering Christ, the actual encounter, and your subsequent response. How you are living out your faith is just as important as the moment of conversion itself. Your faith story includes your life experience and the ways in which God has been woven into its fibers.

A Prayer for You

It's my prayer that this book will encourage and inspire you to explore your own stories—as well as to seek out the stories of others—and to tell them with grace and abandon. It's my prayer that this book will remind you that your life and experiences have great value and that the world needs to hear about them.

It's my prayer that this book will give you permission to share honestly with your family, friends, and community. I pray it encourages you to speak with the confidence that your stories have the power to generate personal connections for you in a way nothing else can. Stories can change us, change the hearts of others, and change the world.

It's my prayer that this book gives you the freedom to speak.

And when you do speak, I expect the world around you to look a bit more hopeful, bright, and good.

PART 1

The Problem:

We're Divided

CHAPTER 1

When the Culture Is Divided

Listen Before You Speak

May the God who gives endurance and encouragement give you the same attitude of mind toward each other that Christ Jesus had, so that with one mind and one voice you may glorify the God and Father of our Lord Jesus Christ.

ROMANS 15:5 – 6

My husband, Erik, and I went through a period when we constantly had the TV on. And when it was on, it was usually tuned to CNN. We'd been called masochists before, and I suppose that subjecting ourselves to the steady hum of the twenty-four-hour news cycle could justify the moniker.

We were smack-dab in the middle of the 2008 presidential election season, so the rhetoric was cranked up and the news network pundits were salivating at the mouth, waiting for the next self-destructive sound bite from the candidates. To suggest the politicians' words were hateful would be no exaggeration.

Today, the cable news network pundits are still at it, the politicians are even angrier, and we in America are *really* more divided than we've ever been. Congress is at a standstill — Republicans and Democrats refuse to work with one another — and some politicians' approval ratings have never been lower.

Facebook users hurl insults and accusations at each other on issues ranging from health care to energy policy to gay marriage. Today, the heated rhetoric isn't just for politicians and pundits anymore, and I'd be lying if I said that election seasons didn't make me want to rip out my hair.

In a few short years, the nation has only become *more* entrenched in ideology, and we're still deaf to the opinions and ideals of those with whom we disagree. It's easy to lose hope, throw our hands in the air, and declare it all lost, believing that, no matter what anyone says, we're *never* going to hear each other.

I've witnessed the polarity of this division firsthand. In the last four years, I've moved from one extreme of American culture — Portland, Oregon — to another — Salt Lake City, Utah. Though I'm grateful the move has opened my eyes and deepened my understanding of the huge cultural and political gaps that exist in our country, I'm still recovering from the whiplash.

Portland and Salt Lake City — Polar Opposites

If you know anything about Portland, you know it's the nation's hub for religious cynicism, rampant liberalism, and dark wash skinny jeans. In Portland, there are more microbreweries and hipsters per capita than anywhere else in the country! (The brewery statistic is real; the hipster statistic is based on strong anecdotal evidence.)[5]

If you're not familiar with Portland, you can glimpse the town's bizarre and unique culture in the sketch sitcom *Portlandia*, starring *Saturday Night Live*'s Fred Armisen.

Because of Portland's population and far-left progressive political leanings, Oregon is a firmly "blue" state on the electoral map. Portland, because of its skeptical nature, is also consistently ranked in the top three least-churched cities in the United States.[6] Proud Portlanders are almost hostile toward conservatives of any kind. There is usually very little room for compromise on economic issues and almost no room for compromise on social issues.

Salt Lake City is unique in its own right. Founded in 1847 by Brigham Young and other leaders of the Mormon pioneers, Salt Lake City is the world headquarters of the Church of Jesus Christ of Latter-day Saints (LDS). About 58 percent of Utah's population is considered LDS. Due largely to the LDS Church's stance on both social and economic issues, the state of Utah is considered the reddest state in the union.[7]

So, to wrap that up for you, it's the polar opposite of Portland.

However, this great mountain city isn't entirely homogenous. Because of the surroundings — which are quite stunning; if you've never visited, you should, if only for the scenery — the state is home to a growing population of devoted outdoor enthusiasts. Because my husband is the general manager of a whitewater rafting business, we've become well acquainted with the dynamics of this community of outdoor enthusiasts on a professional level. It is relentlessly antiestablishment, antireligion, and antiorganized anything.

That Erik and I left Portland for Salt Lake City in 2011 means that for the 2008 election we were in Portland, and for the 2012 election we were in Salt Lake City. But where these two cities have their differences, they also have similarities — the biggest being the inability to bridge the divide between two ideologies. The divisions we see espoused by politicians in our government are a small snapshot of the deeper and broader divisions that have grown and fractured our states, cities, and communities.

What could possibly bridge the gap between these two opposing, cultural forces?

Janelle's Story

During my sophomore year at the University of Colorado in Boulder, I first began to understand the power of story and personal experiences in addressing difficult issues. A single encounter there was like a small seed planted in my heart that would be nourished, years later, when I heard Ann Voskamp trumpet the power of story once again.

Like most college sophomores, I had a firm grasp on what I believed, on what was wrong with the world, and on how I was the one with all the answers to fix those problems. And I'll never forget the moment when everything I knew about opinions and ideologies changed.

I was sitting in a relatively small class — in fact, we all fit around a large conference table. I think it was philosophy of religion. We were talking about the morality of violence and war, and the discussion turned to gun control.

I, being a proud Boulder progressive, stood firmly on the side of increased gun control. In my mind there was no excuse for violence. The conversation was lively, most of us aggressively pushing our agendas, vying for the professor's attention and approval.

Janelle, who was sitting next to the professor, sat silently through the whole debate.

When the discussion had died down a bit, the professor nudged her arm a little and asked her, "You've been pretty quiet. What do *you* think?"

The rest of us went silent as she sat up straight in her chair, eyes firmly focused on some spot on the table in front of her. She recounted a story from her childhood years.

Janelle grew up in a bad neighborhood in Houston, Texas. Her older brother was involved in a gang that pushed drugs to people in the area, and the group had a reputation for being involved in violent crime.

One night, someone came looking for Janelle's brother to exact revenge for something he'd done. Her mom, a single parent, was working the night shift at a gas station, so the older brother was responsible for

Janelle that evening. She was asleep on the couch in the living area when the front door creaked open.

The man who opened the door had a gun in his hand, and it was pointed straight ahead in front of him. Janelle peered over the back of the couch, and the man caught sight of her.

He shouted, "Get out here or your sister is dead!"

The man grabbed her, pulled her over the couch, held her back against him, cocked his gun, and pushed the end of it into her temple. Janelle's brother came around the corner from his room. The man holding Janelle turned his gun toward her brother. Janelle's brother pulled out his own gun from the waistband of his pants, and a short firefight ensued. She fell to the ground and covered her head until it stopped.

When it was quiet, she could hear her brother moaning. Crawling over to him, Janelle discovered he'd been shot twice in the chest. Glancing toward the intruder, she could tell that her brother's gunfire had killed him instantly. Janelle called 911 and curled up next to her brother on the floor while she waited for the ambulance to arrive. The paramedics arrived, but it was too late. He was gone.

Janelle was seven years old.

When she finished telling the story, Janelle continued to stare at the table, showing no emotion at first. We all sat quietly.

When Janelle started to speak again, her voice quavered.

"I think we all agree we shouldn't stand on the side of violence. We should stand for peace. But when it comes to guns and gun control, I feel a little conflicted. It's hard for me to not be in support of our right to bear arms. My brother's right to carry and use his weapon was, I believe, the reason I'm still alive today. I don't know what that man would have done to me. But I also know the intruder had a right to bear his weapon that day too. And his abuse of that right killed my brother."

She sighed.

"It's never as black-and-white as we want it to be," she continued. "Especially when someone's story gets injected into the conversation. All of a sudden, it gets messy. But it's better if it's messy, I think."

Her observation hit me like a punch to the stomach. Everything hurt, and I couldn't really catch my breath. After listening to Janelle, I realized her ambivalent view about gun control — or difficulty in forming one — was valid, and it was shaped by an incredibly intense experience, one I couldn't imagine in my darkest dreams.

We shifted in our seats. We thanked her for telling her story. We picked up the conversation — but something had changed. All of a sudden, we were talking about ways to be proactive when it comes to violence in our communities. We shifted to talking about education and childhood intervention in low-income areas. Our discussion became less philosophical and more practical. The ideas were brought down to earth, and I caught my professor smiling brightly, taking notes and encouraging us on.

Why Listen?

Janelle's deeply personal story moved us from finger-pointing to problem solving, and I wondered even then, *"Can stories really do this? Can stories really change the game?"*

Yes, they can. But only if we're brave enough to listen — then speak.

This culture we live in, this generation I'm a part of, is teetering on the fence between unending apathy and an explosion of frustration. As a result of money's power and influence in our political system, our own ability to influence change at the political level is shrinking. Our voices are being drowned out by the constant chatter and vitriol found on the twenty-four-hour news networks and on the Internet. We're being defined by the sarcasm and wit of Jon Stewart. Most of all, we're being sold the lie that our differences are more important than what we have in common.

I am so tired of the puffed-up, heated rhetoric that's full of empty promises and overgeneralizations. Those of us in the millennial generation have the potential to rise above the apathy we've been labeled with.

Change will start with us.

It starts over coffee, asking a neighbor what her childhood was like.

It starts with knowing the homeless man's name—the one who stands on the corner by your apartment every afternoon—and then asking how you can help.

It starts with getting out from behind a screen and picking up the phone to call a friend you haven't heard from in a while.

It starts in our homes, in our families.

It starts with teaching our kids to listen before speaking.

It starts with turning off the constant chatter of the talking heads on CNN.

It starts with us.

It starts with knowing and sharing our own stories.

It starts when, after listening, we decide to speak.

It starts with understanding our own history and how we arrived at the opinions we hold today.

What has shaped you the most over the years? Is it your relationship with your parents, or the lack thereof? Or maybe you were moved by that series your pastor preached a few years back. Was your worldview impacted when your high school friend went to get that abortion? Perhaps it was sitting with your friend after her son was diagnosed with cancer—and you knew she didn't have health insurance.

Real people stand behind the issues that face our culture and government, but their faces are fading into gray. We're losing sight of them. The only way to bring them back into the forefront of the conversation is to know their stories and be brave enough to tell them. Their stories matter.

I've come to believe that government or institutions aren't going to fix all the problems of the world. And as a believer in Jesus Christ, my allegiance lies with His kingdom first—not with a political party, platform, or ideology. As His follower, I've been instructed to be in this world but not of it. So I live in this torrential tension, which won't fully resolve until He comes back to make all things new.

I can see Jesus' kingdom breaking in, in big and small ways, right here, right now. And part of that transformation is looking past the issue and into the heart of the person.

Jesus cared far more about people than policy.

Jesus Values Our Stories

One of my favorite stories in Scripture tells of a sinful woman who walks into the home of a Pharisee. The boldness of this woman is fierce, but the real game changer is Jesus' reaction to her and how He interprets her actions to those around Him.

Jesus was having dinner at the home of Simon, a Pharisee. The text doesn't tell us what was happening when the woman arrived, but it does say Jesus had "reclined at the table." It was likely that the guests were a group of men, and they were sitting around talking after having finished their meal. Culturally, a woman would *not* be welcome.

Yet, here comes this woman—someone who "lived a sinful life," as the Scriptures describe her—carrying a jar of expensive perfume. She wants nothing more than to be with Jesus, and when her tears wet His feet, she wipes them with her hair. She was a woman, at a table of men, crying at the feet of Jesus with her hair down. She broke almost every cultural expectation in the book.

Simon the Pharisee is appalled, and in other accounts in the Gospels, the disciples are too. But Jesus is a lover of people, not policy. So not only does He welcome the worship of this sinful woman and forgive her sins; He reaches out to Simon and tries to explain the significance of her very personal and vulnerable actions with a story about the gratitude of those who've been forgiven much.*

Jesus valued people's stories. He sat with the prostitutes and tax collectors, and He knew their stories. He also *told* stories of His own, both to address the heart of the matter and the heart that needed tending.

With the power of Christ in us, we have the courage to speak. We have the power to use our own stories and lives to build bridges across the divisive gaps in our culture. It just takes a soft, knowing nudge on the arm as we ask first, "What do *you* think?"

---

*Luke 7:36–50.

WALK OF SHAME
Suzannah Paul

I parked my car in the dim garage downtown. Holding my keys tentatively, I started to pray.

Please Lord, don't let there be protesters. I can't face the protesters. Please, Lord, not today.

If I could just make it down the block, through the unmarked door, and into the elevator, everything would be okay.

As long as there weren't those posters of the mangled babies.

God, the mangled babies.

My weary eyes blinked against the bright sun. As much as I hated the thought of facing picketers, another part of me desired a run-in.

I longed to confront their assumptions.

The street wasn't busy. A few people waited for buses. Professionals walked hurriedly, briefcases in hand. The woman in the tailored suit and sexy heels was not headed to the clinic for her annual exam. Her job, in the skyscraper, surely came with benefits. My husband's and mine did not.

The walk sign lit, and I stepped off the curb, tucking my hair behind my ears. It still smelled like espresso from the chain coffeehouse where I moonlighted. I'd hoped that graduation would confer an end to latte slinging, but the promise of part-time hours with health insurance was too alluring, so I'd tacked another twenty hours onto my workweek.

In a few more months I, too, could see a normal gynecologist without threat of public shaming. I would see a dentist, get new contact lenses, and stop refusing emergency care because I was terrified of the cost. It would be a glorious day.

But today was not that day. As I turned the corner, the clinic door came into view. I hadn't realized I was holding my breath.

Mercifully, the way was clear. Next time I could psych myself up for a confrontation, but today I was grateful for the peace.

Besides, I had to get back to the office soon. The Christian Ed committee couldn't very well meet without their youth pastor.[8]

RESPONSES

What a great post. While I am not the protesting type, I am sure I make assumptions and judge in situations that I shouldn't and your article has made me stop to really think that so many times I don't really know the person and their story (in any situation). Another great reminder to give grace.

Thank you!

Mary

Thank you for writing this. It makes me think about how I might be Judgy McJudgerson, and I need to just stop.

Damsel

Stunned into silence ... and humbled. I say that I won't assume things, yet here I was, as I was reading, assuming. I still have lots of work to do on myself ...

Issy

Although I am unapologetically opposed to the work of PP, knowing its history and the tragedy that takes place within its doors, I understand and agree with your position regarding Christian grace and compassion toward all.

Sarah

When we take time to listen, our eyes are opened to ourselves and to others.

CHAPTER 2

When the Church Is Divided

Sit at the Well

I appeal to you, brothers and sisters, in the name
of our Lord Jesus Christ, that all of you agree with
one another in what you say and that there be no
divisions among you, but that you be perfectly united
in mind and thought.

1 CORINTHIANS 1:10

It was a chilly Saturday afternoon, and I was standing at the kitchen counter. My right hip leaned into the granite; my left hand cradled my growing belly. At thirty-one weeks pregnant, I was starting to feel the discomfort of carrying my daughter. My skin felt thin and stretched underneath the fabric of my teal cotton T-shirt. She was positioned low that day, making my back feel twisted. No matter how I adjusted my stance, I couldn't seem to get comfortable.

I was having an unusually heated conversation with my husband, who was sitting across from me in the desk chair. His hands were loosely clasped together, his fingers intertwined at the knuckles with his elbows resting on the armrests. He sits like that when he's being thoughtful.

The growing tension in the conversation mirrored the tension I felt in my neck and back. When Erik and I disagree, we're usually able to keep our dialogue toned down, thoughtful, and relatively unemotional. I certainly *can* react emotionally from time to time, but I'm usually good at keeping cool under pressure and thinking rationally before I speak. Usually, but not this time. I was pretty hotheaded. Erik, however, was his usual coolheaded self.

I blame my raging pregnancy hormones for my complete loss of emotional stability.

The Day I Exploded

Earlier that day, Erik had spent four hours at a leadership meeting with a group of men who were shaping the elder process for our church. During the discussion they'd addressed the subject of women in ministry. So when Erik returned home, and I asked him about the meeting, we quickly found ourselves in an argument about the current state of women in ministry within our church community. The initial process for selecting an elder board had begun, and women, at that point, were being excluded from the process.

We were about ten minutes into the conversation when it happened.

"Nish, I can't help it I was born a man," Erik said firmly.

That was it.

That one sentence was all I needed to become a wild-eyed, unhinged, fanatical time bomb whose fuse had just burned all the way down. I exploded.

"AND I CAN'T HELP IT THAT I WAS BORN A WOMAN, and that's the WHOLE POINT!" I yelled, my voice hoarse while the palm of my hand slammed down on the cold granite counter.

My eyes started to burn, and tears fell hot down my cheeks.

My volume level startled Rowan, our three-year-old son, who was playing quietly with his Matchbox cars on the floor. His head shot upright, and he gave me a quizzical look, pondering my tone and actions. I looked down at him, my eyes wet and mascara surely running, and gave him a knowing, motherly smile and a wink. It was my feeble attempt to let him know, "Everything is okay, babe," without actually speaking the words.

I felt far from okay.

He smiled back and continued playing while I continued my rant.

"You'll *never* understand the hurt that comes from knowing you'll be treated and seen as less-than in the church simply because of the anatomy you're born with," I explained to Erik. "That there are certain things you're not *qualified* to do because of the way you were born. Because you're a man, you'll never understand the marginalization women feel. Because you're a man, there's nothing you're disqualified from doing. Because I'm a woman, I'm immediately disqualified from doing a whole *list* of things, depending on who you ask.

"And the fact that a group of men were sitting around talking about whether or not women can even be a part of the discussion MAKES ME SICK," I bellowed out, my chest heaving with sobs as I tried to catch my breath.

I was shaking at this point, completely overwhelmed with equal parts emotion, conviction, and passion. For the first time, my personal stance on women in ministry was being challenged. I believe women should be given full equality in all levels of church leadership, meaning they should be able to serve as pastors, deacons, and elders, along with any other official office of authority in the church. It wasn't just a theological conversation anymore. Rubber was meeting the road, and it was hot.

And I already felt burned.

The kind of conflict that divides the church had taken root in my own kitchen.

How Did We Get Here?

We moved to Salt Lake City in the fall of 2011 to be a part of a church plant. I can testify, my right arm raised, left hand firmly on the Bible, that church planting is a messy business. It's beautiful, hopeful, and humbling —but really, really messy.

Now, only a year later, the time had come for our church community to put leadership in place. We had grown so much in such a short amount of time that our community needed some structure and practical direction. It was time to discuss how church leadership is addressed in Scripture, and how it should and would look for our little community moving forward.

A small group of people that included Erik had been handpicked to begin the discussion—all current ministry leaders, house church leaders, and pastors. The discussion would center around the qualities of leadership laid out in 1 Timothy and Titus, as well as in other books and resources. It was a good plan that made a lot of sense: tap the current leaders to discuss future and formal leadership structures and positions for the church.

It had quickly become clear that the people chosen to be a part of the six-month discussion period were all men, even though there were women in our community who led ministries and house churches alongside their husbands.

This made me angry.

At thirty-one weeks pregnant, emotionally charged and already feisty to begin with, this made me Incredible-Hulk angry. The comic-book character becomes a huge, volatile, angry beast when placed under emotional stress. He also turns a gnarly shade of green. So while I didn't exactly turn green and grow big muscles, I did become pretty volatile and angry.

I understood that the reasoning behind the decision to only include men from the beginning was complex. It had a lot to do with governing bodies that helped to oversee our church plant, with deferring to those who provide funding and direction. It also had to do with submitting to our leaders. In my head, I understood all of that, but my heart was torn apart over the reality that half of our church population wouldn't be represented in the leadership discussion/selection process from the beginning.

It all made sense in my head. But my heart? I couldn't ignore the exclusion of my sisters.

On the heels of my rant, Erik was silent for a while, shifting his gaze between his folded hands and my eyes. I stared, teary and frenzied, across the counter, looking for some sign of affirmation, some sign of agreement. He said nothing. He just kept staring at his hands, then me.

I whispered, my voice cracking through the tears, "Babe, if this church doesn't affirm women in leadership, I'm not sure it's a church where I can stay."

I placed my hand on my belly and closed my eyes, praying for composure. I thought of Scout, our daughter-to-be.

"I can't raise our little girl in a church that would disqualify her from serving simply because she was born a female. I just can't do it."

Erik looked at me with loving, sympathetic eyes and gave me a slight smile, finally speaking in his quiet, steady voice.

He began, "Nish, I wish you could have heard some of the stories I heard today. You would think differently about the whole thing if you knew how much prayer, thought, and earnest struggle these men have put into this issue."

I straightened up and wiped my eyes.

He continued, "One of the guys surprised me so much. I had no idea he would be the biggest advocate of feminism and women's equality I've ever met."

Erik smiled at me again, and I turned my eyes downward.

"Nish, you're speaking out of fear and judgment. The way you're addressing this would lead me to think you believe these men aren't thoughtful and prayerful about the issue. They are — very much so. The inequality of women in the church has impacted many of them, and, yes, there's a lot riding on this debate — I certainly agree. But we moved here to be a part of this church, to be a part of a community. We understood the situation going into this, and we came here and submitted ourselves to the leadership that's in place for the time being. We can't let this issue get in the way of our playing an active role in what God is doing through this community in the city. Not yet, anyway."

He let out a heavy sigh, and I let out a shaky one.

I realized it right away — he was right. The exclusion of women in the beginning of the leadership process had become too big and too important to me. In fact, it had become bigger and more important than anything. In failing to look past the issue and into the hearts of God's people, I had broken my own rule: know someone's story before you jump to conclusions.

I later learned that some in the church hoped we'd eventually be able to address the issue as a community and come to a consensus without any outside influence.

But at that moment, I realized I could have invited those guys over for dinner to have a conversation over food. I could have heard how and why they believe what they do and how they arrived at those conclusions. I could have just called these good men on the phone if I'd wanted to. I could have done anything to extend the hand of community and friendship and be willing to listen, but I didn't. I jumped to conclusions instead.

How Did We *All* Get Here?

What had transpired in my kitchen plays out in a multitude of ways every day. On YouTube, loud and angry pastors stand in their pulpits and slap other believers and churches with labels like "heretical" and "unbiblical." They call themselves true, gospel-oriented churches, with the implication that those who are different aren't really following the gospel. This divisiveness rears its head every day in blog posts, in magazine articles, in the pages of books, from the stages of conferences, and behind the closed doors of church leadership meetings. We build these little islands for ourselves with big walls around them to keep out those who are different from us.

The list of "others" is long. And unfortunately, lately, the focus has been on how we are different rather than on what we have in common. It's too easy to get entrenched. We wallow so eyebrow-deep into our opinions, commentaries, and scholarly resources on Christianity that we look right past the Man who gave our faith its name and reason for existence. We do this because it's comfortable. It makes us feel safe. By keeping those who think differently *over there*, away from our safe bubble of security, we give ourselves an excuse to not engage. Or worse, if we do engage, we do so in a hurtful way. In the pursuit of "orthodox" theology, of being *right*, it's far too easy to lose sight of Jesus altogether.

One of my favorite stories about Jesus is found in the gospel of John, when He sits by a well and chats up a Samaritan woman who came to draw water. Since the kingdom of Israel had been divided in 922 BC and Samaria had become the capital city of the northern kingdom, there had been a long-standing conflict between the Jews and the Samaritans. Just over two hundred years after the division, the northern kingdom was taken over by Assyria, and the Israelites were forced out, replaced with five foreign tribes that settled there.*

After many years, the Israelites of the northern kingdom returned and intermarried with the people from the five foreign tribes of Assyria. By the time Jesus came around, Jews thought the Samaritan people were not true Jewish descendants and that their religious practices were not truly Jewish, but rather an unclean mixture of several cultural religions of the day. Jews simply did not have any dealings with Samaritans, and

---

*See 2 Kings 17:13–34.

vice versa. A similar example would be the conflict between Sunni and Shiite Muslims, two sects of Islam that often, and continually, accuse the other of heresy. (Or, on a lighter note, sort of like the Red Sox and the Yankees.)

So Jesus boldly defies the norms of the day in several ways:

- On His journey, He decides to walk *through* Samaria instead of *around* it.
- He speaks with a Samaritan, which was unheard-of in Jewish culture.
- He doesn't speak with just *any* Samaritan; He speaks with a Samaritan *woman.*
- He asks her to draw Him a drink of water. (In Jewish culture, sharing her cup of water would have made Jesus ceremonially unclean.)

I absolutely love that Jesus does this. By simply sitting down, talking, and having a drink of water with this woman, He breaks several cultural and religious norms and extends His hand of grace by offering her knowledge of the greatest gift—living water, or Jesus Himself.

I also love that Jesus knows her *story*. He knows she doesn't have a husband and is living with a guy. He knows she's actually had five husbands in the past. And yet, He sits with her and answers her questions. It's a remarkable picture of Jesus taking the time to know someone across a religious and cultural divide and *engaging*, regardless of what religious folks would think or say about it.

When Jesus sits and speaks with the Samaritan woman, they don't have an argument or a debate over Jewish practices versus Samaritan practices. In fact, they talk only briefly about the differences between their religions. Jesus does so ever so gently, and throughout their conversation, He sets the stage to tell this woman about Himself. Jesus tells her about how she can access living water, the source of eternal life.

The hard and beautiful thing about following Jesus is that we are invited and called to act like Him. Following Jesus is an ongoing, transformational process, and, as believers, we're invited to be a bit more like Him every day. Sometimes that means having conversations that feel uncomfortable.

The heated conversation I had with Erik in the kitchen made me realize I had spent too much time and energy being angry toward the men discussing leadership in our church. I had judged before I had listened, and it was humbling to look back on my words and actions. In pushing for equality, I behaved like a Pharisee — the last thing in the world I ever wanted to be.

The Pharisees were the religious elite of Jesus' day, well versed in Jewish law and traditions, experts on the meaning and interpretation of the Jewish scriptures. Frequently scorning those who disagreed with them, they always made a point of highlighting the ways Jesus was "wrong." And they were often combative. Despite my intentions, this is what I had become—self-righteous, judgmental, arrogant. I was so sure my opinion was "right" and others were "wrong." It's embarrassing to admit it, but there it is.

To pattern our lives after Jesus is to take the time to hear each other's stories, get to know each other, and allow ourselves to be transformed by the "living water" message of Jesus before we debate theology and doctrine, argue over the best way to "do church," or judge a church's flashy lights and programs—or the lack thereof. The Spirit of God is at work in *all* believers, and so many of the divides in the church could be healed if we stopped to listen to the ways in which the Spirit is working in each other's lives.

The person sitting across the theological divide may very well look like a Samaritan to us. But the witness of Jesus has taught us that it makes no difference. What an opportunity we have when we choose to walk through Samaria, sit down, listen, speak, share, and communicate what's most important—our story and the story of God at work to transform lives, refine us, and fill us with His living water.

Jesus invites us to be builders of bridges, and the best way to build a bridge within the church is to act like Him. It's time to go sit at the well and speak grace as we spend time with those who think differently, believe differently, worship differently. Rather than avoiding that person or that group, what if we choose to sit down and talk?

Learning to Sit at the Well

About a month after that heated conversation between Erik and me, the topic of women in ministry was brought up again in our house church, our small group. We have a lot of strong, confident, and independent women in our church, and several of them happen to be in our house church. I proudly count myself among them.

One of the younger women asked me what I thought of it all, and I offered that if our church elders, whoever they end up being, decided that women could not be elders, I wouldn't be able to stay.

"It's a deal breaker for me," I said nonchalantly, with a shrug of my shoulders.

A few eyebrows raised and a few jaws dropped, and I got a few smiles and knowing nods. I imagine it was a bit unexpected to hear a leader of the small group state bluntly that she could see a reason for leaving the church, specifically a church that was just getting started. Surprisingly, I didn't get any criticism or push-back during our meeting, so I just let what I had said stand without any further explanation. Other women chimed in and the conversation continued, and I didn't really give much thought to my answer after that.

One of the young men in that group is named Lucas. He's about five years younger than me, incredibly smart, passionate about the gospel, and a bit of a pain in the backside. (It takes one to know one.) Lucas is terribly witty and can drop one-liners like it's his job. He's become a great friend to Erik and me since we moved to SLC, and it's been a real gift to be in a small group with him over the past few years. Lucas is one of the people in our community who truly makes me a better person.

When Erik and I invited our house church leadership over for dinner one night, Lucas challenged me a bit.

He told me, "The other night, when you said that women not being allowed as elders is a deal breaker for you, I was really bummed to hear that."

I nodded.

He said his heart was for our church to be unified, even though we may think different things about any given issue. He said he couldn't imagine me leaving — that my leaving would "really suck."

I nodded again.

We spent the next hour or two around the table over glasses of wine, discussing women in ministry. We all had differing opinions — some of us more passionate than others, to be sure. We pushed and pulled, we poked and prodded, but at the end of the night we all looked at each other and said, "We really need to hang out more." It was a beautiful sign of graceful disagreement.

I think the world needs a little bit more of this — good discussion over shared meals. There's something to be said for looking a person in the eye when you're talking about sensitive issues. Unlike the anonymity of the Internet, when you share a table with someone, it's impossible to forget you're speaking to an actual human with real feelings. You're forced to treat others as though they're the real people they are. I think the world could do with a lot less Internet and a lot more shared meals.

Even though Lucas and I don't see eye to eye on every issue of gender-related doctrine, I would never in a million years doubt that Lucas loves, values, and cares about me. He places people above his own comfort and puts relationships over disagreement. He's a humble guy, evidenced in the fact that he has allowed himself to be teachable on so much. And knowing that truth has forced me to step back from my clenched-fist opinions on the matter and realize I have some work to do.

The picture of Jesus sitting with a Samaritan woman at Jacob's well perfectly reflects the posture I could have and should have taken on the issue of women in ministry. People who didn't agree with me were, in my book, "Samaritans." In the past, I'd avoided them, wanting to skirt around them and not engage. How dare they think women can't be elders! But as a believer and follower of Christ, I'm invited and called to be changed by Him —by His life and actions. Jesus wouldn't skirt around those who think differently. He didn't. He walked right through Samaria and sat down with a Samaritan woman at the well.

On the issue of women in leadership, I had been unwilling to follow Jesus and sit with those who disagree with me. I had refused to sit at the well.

Lucas chooses to sit at the well.

If I'm brutally honest, I'm still not sure if I can stay in a church that doesn't affirm women as elders. I waver back and forth. But I'm willing to sit down at the table and talk about it, preferably over a nice glass of red.

I want to be like Lucas.

I'm learning how to sit at the well.

FOR WHEN I'VE BEEN AN EARTHQUAKE ...

Jen Hatmaker

When I was two years old, a woman at church gave my mom a copy of *The Strong-Willed Child*. Her keen powers of observation concluded that my mom had a situation on her hands, and it might be best to take it into hand while I was a toddler and she still had a fighting chance at domination.

Let's just say I've always had Big Feelings.

I'm in an interesting season. My Big Feelings have served the kingdom well in many ways. They are part and parcel of Big Passions, Big Ideas, Big Courage, Big Stories. I am a catalyzer, and enthusiasm and conviction are helpful tools for the role. Righteous indignation is a powerful force when dealing with injustice, oppression, abuse. When partnered with discernment, Big Feelings in the hands of the right communicator can initiate important movement.

But Big Feelings can also wound and offend, even unintentionally. Or totally intentionally. As one who tends to buck the system, who often has a problem with The Man (whoever he is), sometimes my prophetic bent unfairly injures. Truthfully, my heart always stands with the Little Guy, the Underdog, the Marginalized, the Misfit, and because I lean toward inclusion and reform and struggle with power paradigms and hierarchies, I sometimes sweep good people into the fray and issue an indictment where one is not deserved.

I've had a couple of direct confrontations in the last six months over this very issue. With an eye toward the outcast and a generous application of my Big Feelings (i.e., Big Public Words), I reinforced some divisions rather than building bridges between the people of God. **What could have moved the body toward unity instead further drove a wedge.**

A couple of mature, godly people I respect pushed back.

It hurt.

I was defensive and felt misunderstood.

I cried.

Then I listened.

I remembered all the times I've been swept up into someone's label, assigned characteristics and opinions and perspectives I never actually held. I've been typecast too, and it is a horrid, helpless feeling, this inability to defend myself against someone else's unmerited statement.

I'm going through a softening, finding tenderness where there was once only indignation. I'm learning a lesson on peacemaking—and I haven't liked it so don't imagine I'm enjoying this season. **But I see that we can accomplish so much more with respectful conversation than burning everything to the ground.** The collateral damage bears consideration; I will answer for it. I do not get a free pass on offensiveness simply because I fancy myself a spokesman for the marginalized.

"The LORD said, 'Go out and stand on the mountain in the presence of the LORD, for the LORD is about to pass by.'" (1 Kings 19:11)

Elijah is going to experience the presence of God, literally manifesting. This is monumental. We are all getting to witness God's physical expression on earth. He had every option available. After all, injustice and idolatry were in play. These were spiritually dark days. Prophets were murdered, covenants broken, altars torn down, righteousness mocked. **If ever there was a time for shock and awe, this was it.** In the face of such societal rebellion and evil, we certainly expect God to rain down blows.

"Then a great and powerful wind tore the mountains apart and shattered the rocks before the LORD, but the LORD was not in the wind. After the wind there was an earthquake, but the LORD was not in the earthquake. After the earthquake came a fire, but the LORD was not in the fire. And after the fire came a gentle whisper." (1 Kings 19:11 – 12)

How can we make sense of this tenderness? How do we interpret such a gentle presence even in the midst of spiritual upheaval? I have so much to learn from this divine moment. God is still powerful, fully sovereign and righteous, yet His approach is healing, soothing, peaceful. The prophet who just said, *"I have had enough, LORD . . . take my life,"* was renewed (1 Kings 19:4).

I want to restore; it is truly the legacy I crave. **I want**

to be a part of a kingdom that heals and soothes, that gives rest to the weary and a safe place to feel God's gentle presence. I sincerely want to build bridges and join Jesus in the work of redemption, not simply deconstruct, inadvertently destroying good work that has already been laid. The gospel is Good News, but sometimes all the Big Feelings make it feel like a civil war, and I'm weary of it.

I'd rather be a peacemaker; there is enough strife on earth already. Although humbling to put my head down and apologize for injuring, for casting some unfair stones, something freed up inside. A hard place became tender and I'm grateful. **There is a way to fight for justice without tearing down the innocent.** The earthquake shatters, yes, but the gentle wind *restores*, and I'd rather be an agent of building up than tearing down.

> *"Your people will rebuild the ancient ruins*
> *and will raise up the age-old foundations;*
> *you will be called Repairer of Broken Walls,*
> *Restorer of Streets with Dwellings." (Isaiah 58:12)[9]*

RESPONSES

Thank you SOOO much for sharing this today . . . This post is extremely encouraging to me, because now I know I'm (1) not crazy and (2) not alone.

Chantal

Oh, if I only had seen this when I was younger ... but God never wearies ... always patient and gentle ...

> *Ro*

Your raw honesty ... encourages me to look at these areas in my own life!

> *Ev*

I'll have to come back and read this tomorrow when I meet that person who, seemingly, couldn't care less that all those children in Africa have no access to education. This is the way of Big Feelings.

> *Rachel*

Your confession has brought words to an inner process I've been dealing with.

> *Jeanine*

Have you been reading my diary? My Big Words/Big Feelings seem to cause this wreckage often, and God is gently restoring me here.

Thank you for sharing the "underground" story and expressing it so well.

> *Bonnie*

> When we sit at the well,
> we discover *the other* there.
> And we find we're not alone.

CHAPTER 3

When the World Is Divided

Raise a Silent Voice

No one can serve two masters. Either you will hate the one and love the other, or you will be devoted to the one and despise the other. You cannot serve both God and money.

MATTHEW 6:24

I thought I understood poverty.

Then I went to Bolivia.

In June 2011, I got a phone call from my friend Matthew Paul Turner, who worked with World Vision, an international aid organization that focuses primarily on releasing children from poverty through child sponsorships. He was working with bloggers and social media professionals, taking them on trips and working on campaigns to promote sponsorships and funding for area development programs (ADPs).

We'd talked a few times previously, mostly me asking a bunch of questions about World Vision and wondering how it was different from all the other child sponsorship programs I had heard about. But on this particular phone call, he asked me about something I wasn't really ready for.

"Nish, we'd love to have you come on a trip, if you can make it. We're going to Bolivia in August. Think about it, pray about it, and get back to me."

I'll be honest. My initial internal reaction was, "Absolutely not."

There was no way I could make it work. It was so soon. The trip was in the middle of my husband's busiest season at the whitewater rafting business. I wasn't sure I could leave my baby son for that long, especially flying to another continent. Every impulse in me wanted to say no to the opportunity.

And yet the thought of making the trip was intriguing. World Vision, and Matthew specifically, handpicked a group of bloggers and social media professionals who communicate to a large audience. We would tour Bolivia with in-country staff and a translator, visiting several ADPs where we would meet families affected by the presence of World Vision in their community, who would then tell us their stories. The goal was simple: go, listen, and write. The stories of the families in Bolivia would connect with our readers, and the hope, in turn, was that the connection would translate into more sponsors for kids in the country.

I remained steadfast in my "no" answer for a long while. Every time my husband would chime in with another reason I should go, I'd respond with hesitancy and reluctance. I tried to convince him it would be too hard for him to take care of Rowan on his own for the almost ten days I would be away. Summers had always been off-limits for travel due to the intensity of the rafting season. I reminded him that the trip to Bolivia would be during one of the busiest times of the year, and I said it seemed selfish for me to go.

Still, he kept pushing, telling me, "We'll make it work; this is too important."

I'd counter by telling him it wasn't *that* important, that surely they could find someone else.

He told me, "They asked you for a reason. You could change the life of a kid. You know that, right? And not just one, but several. One of your readers could sponsor a child, and that kid would immediately be provided a brighter future."

I pouted. I sighed. I sunk my shoulders.

"Fine," I agreed. "I'll go."

So after a whirlwind of getting vaccinations for yellow fever, having my passport updated and expedited, filling out paperwork, hopping on conference calls, and setting up child care, I found myself on the way to Bolivia. I had a job to do — tell stories.

The first week of August came quickly. Before I knew it, I had kissed my son and husband good-bye and boarded a plane to LA, and then one from LA to Miami, where I met the team for the first time. We then boarded a plane bound for La Paz.

I sat in the aisle seat, in a row with my friends Joy and Elizabeth. Matthew was across the aisle from me. Elizabeth was an anxious flyer, so I did my best to calm her with stupid humor as we awaited takeoff. She and Joy struck up a conversation as the plane headed for the runway, and I began to zone out.

I thought of my son. It had been brutal leaving him the previous morning. I remember tip-toeing into his bedroom and sitting on the floor while he slept through the early morning hours. I just stared at him through the slats of the crib, memorizing the curve of his sleepy cheeks and trying to count his eyelashes. It was hard to leave my boy.

I took a deep breath and looked over at Matthew, who returned my gaze.

"Are you okay?" he asked.

I quietly nodded my head and said, "Yeah, I think I'm okay. First big trip away from Rowan, so it's hard."

He gave me that knowing, sympathetic smile that only another parent can give and said, "Of course it's hard to leave him. It's okay to be sad."

My eyes welled up, and I nodded again, turning my head to stare at the seat in front of me.

Rowan, my son, is my firstborn. He has autism spectrum disorder. He's high-functioning and more social than some, so he's more at the Asperger's syndrome end of the spectrum. It's difficult to leave him behind, to disrupt his routine, and trust his care to others. So leaving him to go overseas was a big deal, not only for him but for me too. This was the first time I'd gone on a trip of this length without Rowan. *Am I making the right choice? Was it a horrible mistake to leave? Was I selfish?* All of those thoughts crossed my mind — thoughts I suspected every mother has when leaving her child. Mine, though, always seemed to be amplified, and guilt doubled, because Rowan had so many challenges as a small child, I realized that asking all of those questions was pointless now that I was buckled into an airplane seat on the runway in Miami. I was going to Bolivia, and that was that.

I wiped my eyes and took another deep breath, and the plane took off. Seven hours later, we landed at 14,000 feet in La Paz, where we met Andréa, our World Vision host, and Reyna, our translator. We crashed at a hotel for only a few hours, and the next morning we were on another flight bound for Cochabamba, our home base for the next six days.

Cochabamba

We hit the ground running in Cochabamba, boarding our bus and starting our journey toward Tiraque, a World Vision ADP that had been up and running for about thirteen years. The land was dry and arid, the elevation high. Not much grew in the soil beyond potatoes, onions, carrots, and a few peppers in the warmer areas of the country. It was not a nutrient-rich area, which contributed to the deep-seated problems of malnutrition in children. A group of us visited a nutritional recovery program, where women in the Tiraque community came with their youngest children, babies up to five years old, to learn about proper nutrition for their families. While the women learned different cooking techniques and information regarding food and its nutritional value, the small children attended a pre-school, taught by Victoria.

Victoria was twenty years old and attending high school herself while taking care of her own daughter and teaching these children three days a week. She was a remarkably gifted and inspirational teacher. In my book, any woman who can command a room of twenty or more three-year-olds deserves high praise.

In the dry dirt and grass outside the classroom, we sat in a circle with women eager to tell us their stories, to tell us what their lives looked like during the long motherhood days. Some walked to make sure their younger kids got to school. They walked again to this community center to learn about nutrition while their little ones learned how to read and write in preschool.

We asked them how long it took to walk from their respective homes to this center. Some said thirty minutes; others said an hour; some said almost two hours. One woman, wearing a white sweater, piped up and said if she didn't have to get the kids to walk with her, it would take her fifteen minutes. We all laughed. Bolivian and American, we all understood the universal language of parenting. *Everything takes longer with the kids in tow.*

Those women were so strong. They withstood the absence of their husbands, who often left their wives and children indefinitely in search for work with more pay. Sometimes their husbands moved as far away as Europe, and the only signs of life were rare checks that came in the mail, if they arrived at all. Many of these women suffered physical abuse at the hands of their husbands. Many lived on an income of $450 a year. Despite the conditions in which they'd found themselves, these women were resilient, and their hearts never stopped beating the strong language of love for their children. And they'd found help and support among each other as mothers.

I had heard the term "it takes a village" before, but this was the first time I literally saw a village of women helping each other raise the children of the community. It all started with the children. Everything revolved around the basic needs of the children.

Being in and among these women, these lionesses who cared so deeply about their kids, made me think of the community I'd been blessed with back home. Leaving Rowan behind was so hard, but I was reminded that I don't raise my kids on a proverbial island. We raise our kids in and among other people — people who know and love and care for each others' children, people who know and love and care for each other as we do the hard work of parenting.

Our time came to a close, and we hugged the staff, shook hands with the women, kissed their babies, and boarded the bus back to the hotel. After dinner, I made my way to my hotel room and cracked open my laptop. I downloaded all the pictures I had taken onto my hard drive. I smiled at the photo of the young girl I met — she was wearing a bright pink jacket and a blue knit cap. She was beautiful. The dirt on the edge of her face made the darkness of her eyes stand out all the more. I loved her. The way she stood shyly behind her mother, yet smiling wildly, reminded me so much of myself. I can remember seeing similar pictures of myself as a kid — bright, mischievous eyes, and a warm smile. I looked into her eyes, into her darling face, and realized I didn't care about the statistics anymore. The numbers didn't matter as much. I had my notebook open, and I needed to sit down and type out the story of her mother, the one who walked her two older children to school while she carried her baby boy on her back for fifteen miles, wearing only a pair of toeless sandals. She had broken and callous toes from the daily journey, but no matter, she made the trek so her kids could get to school.

I needed to tell her story.

Maria

The next day, we boarded the bus and headed to another ADP called Colomi. The young girl my husband and I sponsored, Maria, was from Colomi, and I was scheduled to meet her and her family during the trip. Upon arrival, we were quickly shuffled into one of the classrooms in a large, converted warehouse building. It was packed with small chairs and small people, all giggling and smiling and waving.

I saw Maria as soon as I walked into the room. Her bright yellow name tag held her name, but I didn't need to read it to know it was her. I knew that shy smile from the picture I was given when I first chose to sponsor Maria. We made eye contact. She blushed and smiled a wry smile, one corner of her mouth turned up. Just like I do. The half-smirk. I laughed. *Did she know? Did she know it was me?*

Following a presentation, I was invited outside to meet Maria and her parents. This time she looked at me, smiled big and wide, and shook my hand. I told her how excited I was to meet her, and she said, "I was excited too!" I greeted her parents, and they shook my hand in the traditional Quechua greeting. I smiled and told them Maria was beautiful.

Her father beamed, and her mother said, "Yes, she is." She looks just like her mother.

My heart nearly exploded.

Maria told me all about school, and the translator explained that she is very bright. She does extra math problems at home for fun when her friends can't come out to play. She plays basketball and volleyball the most, and she loves to paint and read stories. I told her I like to do all the same things, except the math. She laughed. We sat down on the floor for a little while, and I handed her the gifts I had brought for her—a small basketball, crayons and paper, Ring Pops, a tiara, a stuffed toy, and a Spanish/English *Jesus Storybook Bible*. I told her it is one of my favorite books and that I love the pictures. She sat, mouth wide open, flipping through the pages. I could only watch. After a moment, I explained to her that it's written half in Spanish and half in English, and that I was going to try to work on my Spanish.

She looked at me, a determined smile plastered on her face, and said in Spanish, "I'm going to learn English." I nodded.

She will.

When it was time to leave, I saw the emotion creep up in her parents' faces and flush their dark skin. They both whispered heavily. "Gracias. Gracias. Gracias." Maria's father reached out and grabbed my hand and asked me to send pictures and letters. They wanted to have my family in their home, even though I live so far away. Now my face was flushed. I thought of Erik and how much he would have loved this moment, meeting this man with the beautiful daughter. I thought of Rowan, who would love more than anything to play with Maria and her siblings.

Our family grew that morning. Five people in Colomi, Bolivia, are now part of our family, and we are a part of theirs. We share a common bond — the strongest bond a parent can know on this earth: the love for a child.

"Tell Our Story"

In the bleary-eyed hours of the night back at the hotel, I wrote about meeting Maria and hastily posted it online before I crawled into bed, emotionally and physically drained from being in the field all day. But something stuck with me from that afternoon. I remember sitting with a mother of a boy with special needs. They weren't quite sure what his problem was, but our translator and host both hinted it was probably autism. I asked the mother how I, as a writer, could help—what I could say to the world on her behalf. She very quietly told me, with an interpreter sitting next to me, "Just tell our story. Tell the story of Colomi." I nodded, grabbed her arm, and told her I would. I promised I would. That the people who read my words would know of the people of Colomi. She nodded and thanked me.

I promised.

*

For five days, our team of nine bloggers and a photographer blogged the stories of the Bolivian people for the world to read, in hopes that the stories told would reach the hearts of those who read them—that the stories shared would have such an impact that the reader would sponsor a child and dramatically change the life of a family.

The comments poured in, night after night, day after day, from those who were reading and being impacted by the stories from Bolivia. Children were getting sponsored during our time there. Hundreds, actually. The simple act of sharing stories was changing the lives of children and families in a faraway country. These stories were literally changing the world. It didn't stop with the trip either. A month had passed since my return from Bolivia when I received an email from a mother living in Minneapolis. She explained that my story of meeting Maria's mother connected the dots for her, convincing her that motherhood is a truly universal experience.

Though poverty can feel overwhelming, ending poverty starts with one person, one story.

All we have to do is listen to the stories of those in need. Listen, then tell. Story has the power to advocate.

It can change everything.

Our generation is inundated with calls to social, political, and cultural activism. According to the US Department of State, more than 1.5 million NGOs are in operation in the United States alone. That's slightly more than one NGO for every two hundred people in the US. *Donate here. Give there. Help this cause. Raise more money.* We are inundated with calls asking us to make a difference.

Our generation is suffering from poverty fatigue.

The problem of poverty fatigue isn't with the organizations doing the work. Rather, the problem is with our inability to connect on a deeper level with those in need.

So how do we create a lasting connection to the poor —the ones Jesus called the least of these—in a sustainable, life-changing way? How can we actually work to eradicate the crippling effects of poverty on children, adults, and communities around the world?

Stories.

We need to recalibrate our passions to begin with a person. That happens as we start seeing those stricken by poverty as one of us rather than as *the other*. A common thread of humanness runs through all of us, and we simply need to find the thread that connects us. The problem of eradicating poverty is not about the lack of funding or a marketing strategy. The problem with eradicating poverty is the rampant disconnection between the haves and the have-nots. So when we sit with people and listen to them — about their needs, desires, dreams, expectations, hurts, and experiences — that's when things change.

Addressing poverty in this way isn't simply because it's smart strategy or it makes us feel better about ourselves, or even because it's the most efficient. We meet the needs of those in poverty by hearing from them first, because it's one of the best ways to display the love of Jesus as we know Him in Scripture.

Being Like Jesus

In the gospel of Luke (18:35 – 42), Jesus and those around Him came upon a blind man on the side of the road to Jericho. The blind guy was begging. He had nothing. The crowd surrounding Jesus started to get closer to the man as they walked down the road, and he asked a passerby what was happening.

"It's Jesus of Nazareth," the passerby said with excitement. "He's walking by right now."

And with that, the blind guy sitting on the side of the road called out to Jesus. I mean, really called out to

Him. He'd have to yell pretty loudly, given the crowd of people surrounding Jesus on the road.

And he didn't just yell, "Hey, Jesus!" He called out to "Jesus, son of David," implying that he knew exactly who Jesus was and what He was capable of. "Have mercy on me," the blind man implored Him.

The people in the front of the moving crowd kept trying to hush him, to keep him quiet as Jesus walked by, but he persisted. "Jesus, Son of David, have mercy on me!" You can almost hear the desperation and need in his voice in this portion of text.

Jesus didn't look to someone else in the crowd and ask, "What does that guy want?" Nor did He ask someone else to help the man get what he needed. Jesus stopped and had the man brought right to Him. Right to His face! And Jesus spoke directly to the beggar. He asked him what He could do for him, and the blind man told Jesus he wanted his sight back.

And the man received his sight because he had faith. Jesus healed him Himself. He's God. He could have had any number of His disciples heal the blind man that day, but *Jesus* healed him.

Everyone around Jesus was looking down on the man sitting in the dirt, telling him to be quiet. The text here says they were the ones leading the way, and I imagine Jesus being somewhere in the middle of the crew or possibly near the back. I love the visual of Jesus stopping in His tracks to speak to this man after everyone had already overlooked him. And being the Son of

God, He certainly knew what the man needed before he even opened his mouth to speak. But Jesus asked anyway, "What do you want me to do for you?"

He listens as He looks into eyes and faces. He reaches out to the person—the whole person—and meets their need.

And may it be so with us. When reaching out with our hands, resources, and love to those in need, may we always look into their faces and listen to their stories. Even though it can seem like the voices of those on the margins have been silenced, may we remember that they haven't been. They have stories, lives, and experiences too. Sometimes it's our job to simply be a microphone, offering our volume, influence, and privilege for the sake of those who need it most. I pray we are reminded that those of us with privilege and influence have the ability to share those stories to impact change. Every person's story deserves to be heard and told.

May we be the hands and feet of Christ as we sit and listen and tell the stories of the least of these.

BEYOND BLACK AND WHITE:
YELLOW FEVER AND LETTING GO OF SHAME
Mihee Kim-Kort

Yellow fever:

1. An infectious tropical disease carried by mosquitoes.

2. A term usually applied to white males who have a clear sexual preference for women of Asian descent. [From *Urban Dictionary*]

3. *Feeling shame about one's asianness.* [My definition]

A friend of mine lamented that his girlfriend did not know who he was when it came up in conversation. Something about TMZ and Lil Wayne. I have no clue. He told me he could barely pick his face up off the floor —much less his jaw—when he tried to explain that the story of this little black boy is a huge part of American history, *and how could you not know him???*

But. Would people say that about ... *Vincent Chin*? If I were to ask you to name five Asian Americans who have made a significant impact on American consciousness and identity, could you name someone besides Jeremy Lin or Lucy Liu?

For the longest time I struggled with racial identity. Actually, that's not accurate. I avoided it. I ignored the contradictions I felt in and around me. I pretended nothing was wrong. People often express surprise when I share this piece of my story.

"But, you're Asian! It's not like you're Black or Hispanic." *(Wow. Not even sure where to begin ...)*

"Asians are rich and successful!" *(Have you heard of the model minority myth?)*

"I don't see you as Asian. I see you as American." *(That isn't really helpful.)*

"Your English is so good. There's not a trace of an accent. What's the problem?" *(Sigh.)*

And for the longest time, perhaps the most difficult piece for me to acknowledge was how the church—i.e., white, conservative, middle-class, evangelical Christianity —perpetuated this feeling of *being less.* Trying to put language to this less-ness was next to impossible, and there certainly

Pearl of the Orient. Whore. Geisha. Concubine. Whore. Hostess. Bar Girl. Mama-san. Whore. China Doll. Tokyo Rose. Whore. Butterfly. Whore. Miss Saigon. Whore. Dragon Lady. Lotus Blossom. Gook. Whore. Yellow Peril. Whore. Bangkok Bombshell. Whore. Hospitality Girl. Whore. Comfort Woman. Whore. Savage. Whore. Sultry. Whore. Faceless. Whore. Porcelain. Whore. Demure. Whore. Virgin. Whore. Mute. Whore. Model Minority. Whore. Victim. Whore. Woman Warrior. Whore. Mail-Order Bride. Whore. Mother. Wife. Lover. Daughter. Sister.

Jessica Hagedorn,
"Asian Women in Film: *No Joy, No Luck,*"
Ms. magazine (January-February 1994)

was no space in Christianity to put flesh and blood on it because the illegitimization of it was so subtle and insidious I had internalized it. I was ashamed of my Asianness because it made me not only less of a human being, but a second-class Christian as well. And if I brought up anything contrary to the nice, neat narrative of white, evangelical Christianity, then that was a sin.

The gospel and I discovered each other in the least likely of places—in critical race theory; in feminism; in postmodernism, postcolonialism, poststructuralism; in the social histories of marginalized peoples; in liberation theologies.

Woman Warrior
We are unbinding our feet
We are women who write
We are women who work
We are women who love
Our presence in this world
"The Unbound Feet,"
1979 Performance at the
San Francisco Art Museum

I remember how it felt to read about the internment of Japanese, Koreans, and Chinese (because they all look the same) during World War II. To read about Korean women brought over by US soldiers after the Korean War and being abandoned by their American husbands; abandoned by the US government, which saw those marriages as invalid; abandoned by the South Korean government, which saw them as used goods. To read about the LA riots and the scapegoating and pitting of African Americans against Koreans. To read about how those sorts of riots happened also in Brooklyn and Detroit. To read about Vincent Chin's brutal murder and the injustice that surfaced in the community. People actually blamed him for his own death. People sided with the murderers. People didn't care about the family he left behind or that his fiancée would never know "happily ever after."

The same way this event catalyzed a movement and mobilized Asian Americans in huge ways all across the country, the first time I read these stories I felt them jump-start my own heart and shape my desire to articulate why experiences of racism toward Asian Americans are unique (they don't fit the black/white paradigm of race), and most of all how the church needs to work toward reconciliation with all those who are the Other.

I became angry. Tears-of-rage and tantrumy angry. All the memories of how I was belittled and silenced while my family was ridiculed and stripped of dignity and agency flooded my waking moments. What seemed innocuous and innocent was painful. But what hurt most was when I didn't say anything. Eventually during seminary I was able to work through that anger, which incidentally was a process that occurred during my first year of . . . marriage. To a white man. To another minister like me. To a recent seminary graduate. *To a white man*. I do not recommend this scenario or timing. But eventually I started to embrace. And celebrate. And remember. This month is *Asian American Pacific Islander (AAPI) Heritage Month*. But for the sake of my children, my little *hapas*, every month is AAPI Heritage Month. I want them to know themselves. I want them to love themselves. And I want them to face and counter injustice in all its forms.

I've been healed of my yellow fever—being ashamed and allowing myself to be shamed by the dominant culture. That happened and continues to be nurtured by God, my creator, redeemer, and sustainer, even as I struggle with social and political realities of faith being co-opted by the dominant culture and used as a vehicle of power.

My hope is that yellow fever isn't hereditary, and that my little ones will never have to go through a process of letting go of it. There's too much good to advocate for in them, and not a second needs to or should be wasted on what's destructive, ugly, and mean. Rather, I want us to pour our lives and love into following and trusting that the One called God-With-Us knows in His bones what it means to be rejected as the foreigner (He certainly was from waaaaaaay out of town), stranger, and Other. Because that story matters the most, and as long as it is the one they carry in their bodies, they're going to be stellar.[10]

RESPONSES

Thank you so much for this, Mihee. Powerful writing that makes me wince and want to apologize for any and all ways I have contributed to this pain, this other-ing.

Diana

Woowwwwwwwwwwwwwwwwww! I confess to not knowing either of those people mentioned. Yellow fever: I missed #s 2 and 3 also.

Gary

Mihee, I am sad to say I don't recall hearing about Vincent Chin before this. I was two years old when he died, which may be part of it. But your question about naming five Asian Americans who have made an impact is a good one. One I'm not sure I can answer and that shocks me. I don't know if I could come up with five names for any race or cultural category, but this is definitely something about which I want to be better informed. I have some work to do. Thank you for sharing this part of your story.

HopefulLeigh

This says so much, and thank you for your candor ... This made me ache for a real and full conversation with you.

Sharon

> **When we listen to voices**
> **that have been silenced,**
> **we become more**
> **fully human.**

PART 2

The Solution:

Story Changes Hearts

CHAPTER 4

Claiming Our Unique Gifts
God's Kingdom Is Built

We have different gifts, according to the grace given to each of us. If your gift is prophesying, then prophesy in accordance with your faith.

ROMANS 12:6

I was lying on my stomach on the rough and irritating carpet of the youth group room at the Nazarene church down the road from my neighborhood. My sweaty hair was pulled back into a ponytail, and I was still wearing my spandex shorts and a jersey. I'd come straight to youth group from a volleyball tournament. I was a junior sitting with the other junior girls in a circle, some of us lying on the floor and others sitting cross-legged against the wall. All of us held a slim packet of paper in front of us and a pen. We were filling out a spiritual gifts evaluation. Our youth pastor had just taught us a lesson about the spiritual gifts listed in Scripture, and then he handed out a packet full of questions to help us determine what our own gifts were.

Back in the day, I was a huge fan of personality tests. Okay, who am I kidding? I'm still a fan of personality tests (Myers-Briggs: INTJ). But at sixteen, completely unsure of who I was, filling out personality tests was a way to help me get a grasp on my identity. They would identify what I was good at and what I should be doing with my life in the future.

I have a little bit of a type-A, controlling streak. So I lay there on the scratchy carpet, circling my answers diligently, reading each question twice, just to make sure I'd read them correctly. Thirty minutes passed, and I was the last to finish. We calculated our scores, tallying them to reveal our top spiritual gifts. I pulled my pages back into their rightful order, straightened out the stapled corner, and put my pen on top of the paper.

Then the youth pastor invited everyone in the group to share our top-scored gift. Angela, the volunteer leader in our group, asked my friend Macy to go first. Macy grabbed her sheet and sat a little bit taller while the rest of us positioned ourselves to listen.

"My top one was teacher," she said with a small smile.

Everyone started nodding their heads in agreement.

"I can totally see that in you!" Dani said from across the circle.

Macy smiled and looked down at her paper. "It felt like it fit me, you know?" We nodded again.

Our leader then asked Ashley, to Macy's right, to share.

"Mine is faith."

The nodding continued as each person went around the circle to share their gift. And with each person, I started to get more and more uncomfortable. *Why can't anyone else have a weird one like mine?* I thought to myself. I kept my eyes down on my paper. My turn was getting closer, and I'd made up my mind. There was no way I wanted to tell this group of girls what mine was. I'd just gotten invited to Macy's house for the first time last week, and it had taken so long to feel like I was welcome in this youth group. I wasn't about to give that up and become the *weird* one. What should I do? My palms started to sweat, and I rubbed them against the tops of my thighs.

Angela looked at me. It was my turn.

"Nish, what's your top spiritual gift?"

I fumbled my papers a bit to make it seem like I was referencing my answers.

"Mine was hospitality," I said quietly, avoiding eye contact with the rest of the circle.

"That makes *total* sense!" Macy said.

"That totally suits you," someone else mentioned.

I offered up a shy smile and said thanks. It was someone else's turn now, thank God. I looked down at my paper and snuck a glance at the last page, where my top gifts were circled in a scratch of red ink.

Prophecy and Pastoring.

I know there are a lot of differing opinions and theological arguments about tests and questionnaires having to do with spiritual gifts. Many people swear by them, while others brush them off as insignificant. Personally, I think they're a good starting point for reflection. For anyone who has very little to no understanding of these gifts, the surveys can be a good way to dip their toes into the water and start a prayerful journey toward discovery.

Now years later, my results have proven to be accurate. And yet, most days, I still sit with my gifts much like I did when I was sixteen — hesitantly and fearfully. Not only have I seen the gifts manifested in myself over the years through the guidance of the Spirit; I've also had several people close to me, including my husband, affirm that prophecy is indeed my strongest gift.

I still wonder how I might be used for the good of the church and for the good of what God is accomplishing in the world. In the midst of the everyday hustle, it's easy to forget about things like *purpose* and *story* and *vision* and *kingdom*.

Most of us are just trying to get through another day. We're clocking hours at a temp job at a legal firm. We're teaching Spanish to high school students. We're putting in another day at the office, making more copies. We're doing another load of laundry, changing another diaper, wiping another pair of dirty hands. We're making another double-shot latte. When there are bills to pay, mouths to feed, and a boss to please, thoughts of things like gifts of the Spirit can take a backseat. Trust me — I get it.

My days are filled with children's temper tantrums, sweeping crushed Goldfish crackers off the couch, and scraping peanut butter off the sandwich bread because *how dare I put peanut butter on his sandwich*! My days are spent mixing another bottle of formula, moving sharp objects out of the reach of little hands, and watching the movie *Wreck-It Ralph* for the billionth time. I'm constantly stepping on Legos, slipping on Matchbox cars, and dodging incoming monster trucks. My spiritual gift of prophecy doesn't come in handy, nor do I even have the time to think about it ... unless you count the instances I've envisioned my child tripping over the random shoe he left in the hallway—and this prophecy coming true every single time.

The truth is, God has gifted each of us in unique ways. Whether we have the time to *think* about it is, frankly, irrelevant. We have been gifted, and God has instructed us to use our gifts and talents for the good of the kingdom. How God has gifted each person is a significant part of both our own story of transformation and redemption and the story of His work in the world:

> For just as each of us has one body with many members, and these members do not all have the same function, so in Christ we, though many, form one body, and each member belongs to all the others. We have different gifts, according to the grace given to each of us. If your gift is prophesying, then prophesy in accordance with your faith; if it is serving, then serve; if it is teaching, then teach; if it is to encourage, then give encouragement; if it is giving, then give generously; if it is to lead, do it diligently; if it is to show mercy, do it cheerfully.
>
> ROMANS 12:4–8

Jesus taught us to pray, "Your kingdom come, your will be done, on earth as it is in heaven" (Matthew 6:10). And though God's kingdom is more fully realized on earth when each of us is fulfilling our unique purpose, many of us don't know where to start. I certainly get so entrenched in the everyday that serving in any other capacity feels like just another thing to do, another thing to check off my list, another something piled onto my plate.

So we carve out space in our communities to tell the stories of people using their gifts for the benefit of the church, for their neighbors, and for the kingdom. This is what empowers us to think creatively about our gifts, and we get new ideas through the sharing of stories and experiences. I never would have considered blogging or writing books as a means to exercise my spiritual gifting four years ago. But soon after my son was born, I met another woman with the gift of prophecy as it's expressed in the New Testament. She is a mom of three children, all of whom were then in middle and high school, and she is gifted—or maybe *burdened* is the right word, now that I think about it—with an outlet for writing books. She is now powerfully and prophetically speaking to the church on matters of gender and justice, calling them to repentance and action. It was remarkable to watch and extremely valuable to learn new ways I might use my gifts as I received her story.

So I want to challenge you to pay attention to your own gifts and those of others.

First, if you don't know already, find out what your spiritual gifts are. You can certainly take any of these spiritual gifts inventories as a starting point. I think these tests, while not conclusive or highly nuanced, still provide a worthwhile start by asking some great questions. And one of the best ways to identify your gifts is by asking those who are closest to you. These people are able to see you at your best and your worst, in and out of ministry or your vocation.

Second, once your gifts have been identified, connect with two different types of people. The first person should be someone who shares your primary spiritual gift and who has, preferably, lived a bit longer than you have. Sit with that person, buy them a cup of coffee, and ask them how they use their gifts to benefit the church and the community. Listen and take notes. Ask for prayer and guidance. Be a little vulnerable and share some of the fears, insecurities, and challenges you face regarding using your gifts.

The second person should be someone who has a completely *different* gift from yours. Find someone who has a gift you admire — a gift that is not only different from your own gift but *wildly* different. Ask them the same kinds of questions about their gift. Sometimes we need a completely different perspective, and we have much to learn from those whose gifts are different from our own.

I remember meeting with and listening to my friend Tina talk about her gift: evangelism. I am *not* a gifted evangelist. In fact, I'll be honest—sharing the gospel even with people I know can be downright terrifying. I'm much better at talking to people who've already subscribed to the Christian faith. But my friend Tina? She's incredible at evangelism. It's a true gift.

Tina has been an outgoing and helpful person her whole life. She was always the one to say hi to other kids at the park, always the one to help someone when they fell down, always the one to introduce herself at parties to random people she'd never met. She's never been afraid of social environments, and she's a natural at connecting people and at networking. Tina is one of those people who feels like your best friend after only five minutes of talking to her. She's warm and inviting. She has a huge smile and is one of the kindest people you'll ever meet.

Tina became a Christian during her freshman year of college. A cute, outgoing guy in her chemistry class leaned over and slid a flyer across their lab table. It was an advertisement for a big back-to-school bash put on by a local campus ministry.

He winked at her and told her, "You should come out. It'll be fun."

Tina turned bright red and said she'd show up that night.

"I was absolutely amazed that this guy talked to me, let alone invited me to something," she confided to me.

We laughed as she told me about how she made her way to the event, hanging with the guy from chemistry class and introducing herself to everyone in the room. It was at this event that Tina heard the gospel for the first time, and a few weeks later, she became a believer —with the chemistry guy having led her toward faith.

After hearing and believing the gospel, Tina began telling everyone she knew about it. Within three months, twenty-seven other people were coming to this ministry with her on a regular basis, all choosing to give their lives to Christ. It was clear that Tina was blessed with the gift of evangelism. She ended up marrying the guy from chemistry class, and together, they've been on staff with this campus ministry for the last eight years.

"I've always been outgoing and easy to get to know. I know that about myself," Tina told me over coffee. "In my heart, I knew they were good qualities to have, but I've always questioned it. I never knew why I was the way I was. Then I became a Christian and received the Holy Spirit, and it all made sense. I was made the way I was to reach out to others, to tell them about Jesus."

Meeting with Tina and hearing about her gifting, about how she's been made a certain way with a certain personality, opened my eyes to my own life, my own gifts. I came to realize there were things about myself that had been there all along. I've always been blunt and straightforward. I've always carried a deep empathy for others. I've always loved guiding and shepherding people to something bigger than themselves. But I'm not sure I would have ever noticed this without talking to Tina.

Sitting with Tina in that brightly lit coffee shop over a couple of lattes was a time that brought our friendship closer. In fact, we shared some things about ourselves that we had never shared before. I'm so thankful I reached out to her and simply asked, "How'd you figure out you were meant for evangelism?"

As you begin to connect with those whose gifts match yours, and with those whose gifts don't, I pray that the stories and experiences shared between you and others will help build relationships in your community and draw you into closer and more intimate friendships. I expect you'll also glean some new ideas about how to use your gifts.

If we share one body, it's probably best that we get acquainted with one another, don't you think?

WITH TINGLING FINGERS AND SHAKY VOICE, I SPEAK OF HEALING

Megan Tietz

There was a crowd gathered around her, so I only saw her legs and feet there on the dingy, dirty floor of our Goodwill store.

We were running late, my youngest daughter and I, and I was rushing to the checkout line when I saw her laid out there. Someone was on a cell phone, calling 911. Those standing nearby were telling each other what they had seen, that she seemed to know she was blacking out, that she slowly and carefully slumped to the floor. Weeks have gone by, and I can't shake the image of her feet, one neatly lying on top of the other, both armored in white orthopedic shoes, legs demurely covered by navy blue polyester.

I can't shake how I stood in the checkout line at the Goodwill store with my heart racing, thinking, *What if I did it? What if I just went over to her, put my hands on her, and prayed?*

But I didn't. I paid and walked out the door as the paramedics rushed in.

***

Many, many years ago, my now-husband was my then-boyfriend, and we were in a Sunday school class together. We filled out surveys meant to diagnose us of our spiritual gifts. I tallied my score and discovered that according to this test, I had the gift of healing. *Hummph*. What a dud. What a disappointment. Healing. It's one of the *temporary* spiritual gifts, right? I was a few semesters from graduating with a degree in education, and I had been hoping I would score highest in teaching. I quietly tucked the defective spiritual gifts inventory in the back of my Bible and, compliant Southern Baptist girl that I was, promptly forgot about it.

Until.

Until years later when one of my best friends sent me a biography on Sister Aimee. Aimee Semple McPherson founded the Foursquare Church and was an outrageously popular faith healer in the United States in the early twentieth century. Her life story was fascinating, and I inhaled the book in a few days. As the biographer explored the beginning of Sister Aimee's healing ministry, he wrote that when she prayed for a person's healing, she visualized the healing taking place as she prayed. In her mind's eye, she could see the wound closing or the bone straightening or the eyes seeing.

That stopped me in my tracks.

That was precisely how I had always prayed when I prayed for a physical healing. No one had ever taught me or instructed me in that; instinctively, though, I would imagine a cancer shrinking or a throbbing pain being soothed into nothingness. It never occurred to me that there was any other way to pray for healing, but at the same time, I had never seen anyone describe what it felt and looked like as precisely as Sister Aimee's words did.

It gave me pause, but not much else. It was all *a bit Pentecostal* for me.

* * *

And so, I don't know how I got from there to here. I don't know how I went from fleeting curiosity to cautiously convinced. About a year ago, I felt God stirring in my heart about the healing issue. I began to wonder, *What if that spiritual gifts inventory wasn't a fluke? What if healing wasn't a temporary gift?* **What if I had the gift of healing?**

As preposterous as that feels to write, it felt even more ridiculous to say it out loud. At first, I confided only in my husband and my parents that I was thinking about these things. Eventually, I told only a few of my closest friends. No one laughed out loud. No one scoffed or rolled eyes or patted me on the head.

And then things started to get *weird*.

Like the time I put my hand on my brother's shoulder, and I could feel a warmth move from my fingers to his skin, and I prayed that an old injury that was causing him excruciating pain would be healed. And now it doesn't bother him anymore at all.

Like the time I gathered with a small group of women to lay hands on and pray over a sweet sister who had been diagnosed with breast cancer. As soon as my hand touched her, I felt my hand and arm, from my fingertips to my shoulder, set fire with heat and tingling and through tears I prayed. She is now in remission.

Like the time my oldest daughter had a serious bout with the flu, and her temperature soared to 104 and wouldn't stay down with medicine, and I kept my hands on her and mumbled pleading prayers for what felt like an entire night, and in the morning, she was better.

* * *

So why did I walk away from the lady on the floor of the Goodwill?

The truth is, I have no idea what I'm doing here. And it scares me. And I've been praying for healing for someone for my whole entire life, and she has not been healed. And I know, I *know*. I know that ultimately all sickness and all brokenness can all be used for God's glory. I know that He chooses to heal in ways that do not seem like healing to us. But there has to be something there, or why won't God leave me alone about it? Because, trust me, I'm on the receiving end of Crazy Eyes enough on my own without purposefully seeking out something supernatural and strange.

I'm only a few pages into this chapter of the story of my life. I can barely finish a sentence; I have no idea what the next paragraph will reveal. So would you pray for me? Pray that I'll seek and find His Truth in this. Pray that I'll have the courage and compassion to kneel on the cold floor of Goodwill next to someone who needs prayer. Pray that as I find my way on this path, I pursue always and only the Healer above all.[11]

RESPONSES

Loved this! Encouraged me to passionately pursue my gifts!

Dianne

Megan, I've got a heart for prodigals. I have a prodigal prayer journal with names. As I write out my prayers, I, too, have visuals. I see them walking Home, finally seeking out Papa and His embrace of grace.

Will pray for you. Thank you for your post and your heart.

Rebekah

This is so great! I am forever leaving an encounter with someone thinking, "Wow, why didn't I pray for that person?" I long to have a greater awareness of the Spirit and to be a part of bringing the kingdom. I am so excited for you—and thank you so very much for sharing.

d.l.

I am *so* glad and happy and excited that you posted this. I have felt the pull of healing for a long time now too . . . I just felt it within, like you said. . . . You are not alone. We are beginning to witness what we were intended for. God bless.

Alisha

> **As we claim our unique gifts,**
> **God's kingdom is built.**

CHAPTER 5

Vulnerably Offering Our Stories

God's Kingdom Is Blessed

If you want to reach this generation and every
generation to come, go first with your story and give
everyone around you the gift of going second.

JON ACUFF

Then Jesus came to them and said, "All authority
in heaven and on earth has been given to me.
Therefore go and make disciples of all nations,
baptizing them in the name of the Father and of the
Son and of the Holy Spirit, and teaching them to
obey everything I have commanded you. And surely
I am with you always, to the very end of the age."

MATTHEW 28:18 – 20

I haven't always loved the church. In fact, I hated it for a good while.

I know "hate" sounds harsh, but when your heart gets racked by bitterness, cynicism, and anger, "hate" is probably the best word for how it feels.

Hatred and anger were just outward symptoms of something else. I had been burned by the church, and the people who hurt me the worst were the ones who proclaimed Christ as their king. They masked their actions in what they called faith, righteousness, and a sort of piety that made me want to breathe fire.

It's the sort of burn that one doesn't easily forget. It's difficult to find healing, and calluses form, resulting in a hardness that's unlike any other. I've been hurt by a lot of people in my past (and lest anyone think I'm innocent, I know I've done my share of damage too), but the ones that hurt the most are inflicted by other believers.

The wounds eventually turned to scars, and the

tissue around my heart became calloused and hard. But it didn't take much to reopen the wounds I'd never allowed to heal. Those scars had become a road map to a dark place of cynicism and even contempt toward the church. That's where I set up camp. It was comfortable, and I found a lot of friends in that place—although I didn't recognize that that's where I was living. I still went to church and led Bible studies and youth groups, and we even moved to another state to be part of a church plant. All the while, I sat content in my festering anger.

Jenna

It was early spring. The cherry blossoms were starting to bloom around Salt Lake City. I was walking through Liberty Park at a leisurely pace, and the breeze swept my hair across my sunglasses. I'd made a phone date with a faraway friend on this morning—at a time when I knew I could get someone to watch the kids for a while. When my phone rang at ten-thirty sharp, I answered immediately.

Jenna (not her real name) and I laughed, joked, asked about each other's kids, and laughed some more. This friendship was a long-standing one, and even though we hadn't talked in months, it felt like I'd just been in her living room yesterday. We started talking about church, and she told me about a sermon series she'd been preaching. As she shared, I got quiet. When it was my turn to talk about church, I gave short, one-word answers. When I did expand on a few thoughts, they were pretty negative.

"You sound bitter," she said after a long pause.

"I suppose I probably am," I replied with a nervous laugh.

Jenna let out a long sigh.

"You should figure that out, and quick. It's eating away at your ability to be joyful and love people."

I told her curtly that what she said felt a little harsh, and I could almost hear her shrug her shoulders nonchalantly through the phone.

"Do you enjoy going to church?" she asked. "Do you enjoy being with other believers? I'm going to guess that you don't."

She was right. I didn't like going to church, and I didn't like being around other Christians.

Erik and I had made our move from Portland to Salt Lake City two years earlier when our dear friends, Kyle and Joy Costello, asked if we would move to Utah to help start an urban church with them. Now, two years later, I was still feeling bitter and cynical.

The breeze blew even harder, and I had to stop to put my hair into a ponytail so I could see where I was going. I set the phone down on a bench along the walkway, pulled my hair back, ran my hands over my face, and took a deep breath.

I suddenly felt very alone.

Bitterness and anger give the illusion of affinity. It

had been easy to find other people who were bitter and angry toward the church. But in reality, bitterness and anger are a darkness that can swallow a person. And Jenna had noticed that I'd been swallowed.

I picked up the phone again and continued on my walk, and we changed subjects. By the time I made my way back to the car, we had hung up—and I was alone with my thoughts.

I was thinking that I was tired of being cynical, angry, and bitter.

Over the course of the next year, I became very close with a group of women I knew online through blogging and social media. There are about twenty of us altogether, and we still speak with each other almost every single day. We've vacationed together. We've walked through pregnancy, childbirth, and parenting together. When I found out I was pregnant with Scout, they were among the very first to know. Say what you want about relationships that begin online, but I'm here to tell you that these friendships are the real deal. These relationships have been, for me, intimate, honest, and true.

I logged onto Facebook one afternoon and saw that someone had linked to a post by teacher and author Beth Moore, who wrote, "There's a bigger issue in the body of Christ than immorality. It's hatefulness. If the greatest priority Christ assigned to us was love, the gravest offender is hate ... I love the body of Christ. I don't want to get cynical. I don't want to sit around and hate the haters or I become one. But this morning I just want to say this. We can love each other better. Let's do. People have enough hurt. Let's be careful with one another."[12]

The truthfulness of her words pierced me that afternoon. Though I was sitting quietly in my office chair, it felt like I'd just done a full-body workout. I was out of breath, as if the wind had been sucked right out of my lungs. It took me a good ten minutes to recover, to gather myself enough to understand why her words were affecting me the way they did. It became crystal clear: I was not loving others.

In fact, I *hated* the church.

I clicked over to the community board where all my girlfriends posted. We had created a private group so all of us could interact daily. I typed frantically, saying that I needed to step back for a while, that I needed to confess that I hated the church, that I wasn't loving others well. I linked to Beth Moore's blog post and explained that her words prompted something deep in me, that I needed to figure some things out. As I expected, they were all gracious and understanding.

My friend Amber Haines told me, "You need to talk to Seth."

Seth

Seth is a fellow writer, a good friend, Amber's husband, and a wise man. He's been through the ringer when it comes to church hurts and betrayals, so I knew Amber was right. I knew bits and pieces of his story but not the whole thing.

He reached out to me only a day later and said gently, with his thick Southern drawl, "I'd love to tell you about how I hated the church for a long time, then learned to love it."

I took him up on the offer, and we started a conversation over the phone the next morning. I'd opened the blinds to let the morning light in and was sitting in the big overstuffed chair in our living room at the front of the house. Rowan was snuggled on the couch watching a movie, and Scout, my newborn daughter, was fast asleep for her morning nap in the other room. With my hot coffee in hand, I answered the phone.

Seth immediately started walking me through his whole story—deception and dishonesty from those in ministry, struggles with vocation, the ups and downs of marriage. Passion had turned to disillusionment, which turned to cynicism, which turned to redemption. He spent nearly an hour telling me his personal story, which was nothing short of brave. Near the end, Seth shared his revelation.

"It took me a long time to realize it, but I finally told my friend I hated the church. He said that if I hated the church, then I hated Jesus, and I told him I didn't want to hate Jesus anymore. It turns out I'd made an idol out of the church. And when you idolize anything that isn't Jesus Himself, it's gonna fail you."

In his own way, Seth had placed the people in the church as the thing to believe in, the thing to count on, the thing to put his hope in. But the problem with that is that people, regardless of their position in leadership, regardless of their celebrity image or their socio-economic status, are just people. They're humans who screw up, mess up, and blunder. So, naturally, when we put our hope and faith in people, they're going to fail us at one point or another. That's the problem with idols. They can't be relied on for too long.

I sat with Seth's idolization of the church for a long time. Had I done that too?

I was thinking about his story while I was folding the seventh load of laundry that afternoon. I held the T-shirts under my chin while I folded the arms in, and with every piece of cotton added to the pile, I felt a tightening in my chest. I grabbed the stack of Erik's shirts and placed them in his middle drawer. I slid it shut, and with its quiet thud I knew I needed to confess.

I'd made an idol out of the church, and she'd fallen from her high shelf in my heart and shattered. The problem wasn't that she fell. She was never meant to be up there in the first place.

It turns out I confused wanting to be like Jesus with actually being Jesus. Trusting in the people who hurt me was my version of the former, but I treated them and held them as the latter. Did they wrong me and hurt me? Yes. But should I have ever put my hope, faith, and trust in them rather than Jesus? Absolutely not. I hit my knees right there in my dimly lit closet, and I didn't know what else to do but push my face to the floor, my cheek resting on the pile carpet. I cried. Hard.

I'm not sure I'll ever fully understand the Holy Spirit, but after some time on the floor shedding big fat tears, I felt peace and reassurance and was ready to get up off the floor. When I stood up and wiped my eyes, I felt new and whole. Restored. It was an odd feeling, this desire for repentance. Never before had I wanted to get up and run 180 degrees in the opposite direction of who I'd been.

That evening, Erik and I sat on our white-railed front porch with a cold drink while our four-year-old Rowan played and flirted with the college girls who live next door. We live on a lively street, and we have an incredible view of the Wasatch Mountains from our porch. I was sitting in one of the chairs with my feet propped up on the railing, looking out at the mountains that were turning purpler with every passing moment of the sunset. Cars were buzzing by and slowing down, pulling into the grocery store parking lot across the street, while we sat on the porch, listening to Rowan laugh.

I told Erik everything—the hatred, the anger, the cynicism, the idolization, the crashing and burning, the turning toward repentance. I told him I was different, and the tears flowed again.

Then he asked, "Well, what are you going to do?"

I said I wasn't sure, and he immediately pointed me to prayer.

And so, for the first time, I was praying for those who'd hurt me, and I was praying for those I'd hated. I was praying for the church. And I have been reminded of the power of the gospel as I've reached out to those on the other side of some of the bridges I'd torched with my bitterness and anger and was offered a forgiveness and love I didn't deserve.

I don't have it all figured out. I'm still trying to fumble my way through it, and I'm learning that repentance is a daily, minute-by-minute choice. Day by day, I'm leaning into it, being reignited by a personal revival. And by the grace of God, I just might see a full recovery from cynicism after all.

My move toward repentance, my turning toward Jesus in my anger and cynicism, was prompted by the bravery of one man. He was willing to lay out on the table his own story of cynicism, anger, and bitterness for me to see, for me to hear, for me to be changed by his telling. Seth's journey is what ignited one of the most significant moments in my life as a believer. I'm not sure I ever understood what repentance meant before I experienced it that day. When Seth told me he'd made an idol out of the church, everything clicked, and I hit my knees. The rest is history.

Seth's own story of repentance brought me to the feet of Jesus, and I'm a more devoted disciple because of it. Seth's story changed my life.

Laurie

I met Laurie almost two years ago. She was wearing acid-washed jeans and an old, black Van Halen T-shirt on a hot day in May. Her short, black hair was stuck to her forehead with sweat, and she kept her eyes down, for the most part—unless a car drove by or someone walked past. When the occasional breeze blew, she would raise her head, close her eyes, and let the sunshine warm her skin a bit more. She stood on a small patch of grass in front of the Smith's grocery store across the street from my house, her trusty cardboard sign in hand that asked for "spare change—every little bit helps!"

Laurie and her husband, Mike, took turns standing on the curb. From what I could tell, this was their first day at this location. Because we live across the street from a grocery store in downtown Salt Lake City, I make the arduous one-hundred-yard journey across the street at least once a day.

This particular time, I had my reusable bag. I was going to grab some food for dinner. Laurie had her back to me when I walked by, but I made sure to turn and smile at her and say hello.

"Hey there!" she said, cheerfully.

"How are you doing today?" I asked.

"Oh, I'm just great! How are you, sugar?"

I told her I was doing well, and I asked if I could get her anything to drink from inside. Her voice was raspy.

"Boy, I'd sure love a Pepsi."

I nodded and turned, hollering over my shoulder, "You got it! Be right back."

I quickly gathered what I needed for our spaghetti dinner, opened one of the small soda refrigerators in the checkout line, and grabbed a Pepsi—the kind with real sugar. The real stuff is always better than the kind with high fructose corn syrup, in my opinion. I paid with a quick swipe of my card and headed back outside. I pulled the Pepsi bottle out of my bag as I approached her.

"Here you are, ma'am!" She looked a bit shocked.

"Ma'am?" she asked incredulously. "That's mighty proper of you!"

I explained I was raised in the South and that those manners never really leave you.

She laughed and replied, "Well, I haven't been called ma'am in quite some time. That felt nice. And may God bless you and keep you, and may His face shine upon you for buying me this Pepsi."

I shuffled my feet a little and told her, "Oh, it's no problem." Then I asked her, "*God bless you and keep you?* That's an old blessing found in Scripture. I haven't read that one in a while."

She smiled, pulled a small Gideon's Bible out of her back pocket, and said, "Oh, it's one of my favorites. It's so beautiful, isn't it?"

I nodded and asked, "When did you become a believer?"

And Laurie dove into the story of her conversion, which had taken place only two years prior.

When I asked Laurie what prompted her to believe the gospel, she simply told me, "Someone else told me their story of conversion. Someone like me. She was kicked out on the streets, man. Living out of a shopping cart. But she had the Light, man. She had it! We became such good friends. She's still one of my best friends. We knew each other for a long time, a few years, before I finally asked her why she was so different from everyone else. She told me she had hope—and that was something I had been looking for, for a long, long time. Yes—hope."

I was gripped by Laurie's story.

She continued, "Kim is my friend's name. When we finally became good enough friends and I felt like I could trust her and she could trust me, Kim told me her hope came from the Lord. She told me how God loves those who are down on their luck, that He loves us the most. She showed me the places in the Bible that talked about us—the poor and the homeless. It took me a while to understand, because for so long, love and care meant money and safety. But Kim reminded me that love isn't very safe at all."

I stood there on the curb for a minute, trying to choke down the lump in my throat. Laurie walked over to a car that had slowly approached her—the passenger handing her two one-dollar bills.

"Thanks. God bless you, sir," Laurie spoke loudly.

She continued as she walked back toward me.

"There's nothin' more dangerous and scary than layin' your crap out for someone else to see, to tell them your whole story in hopes that they'll see the Truth in it."

Laurie wiped her hair off her forehead and smiled.

"But Kim did. She laid it out, man. She became my friend. She told me everything, and I couldn't look away. She told me all the things she'd done in her life and how God rescued her. It was the best story I'd ever heard. How do you say no to that? I wanted to be rescued too."

I stopped suppressing my tears at this point and just let them roll down my cheeks.

"Honey, why are you cryin'?"

"What you said. It's just perfect. It's just so true," I told her.

She smiled at me again. "It sure is, honey."

The breeze blew. Laurie lifted her head up, closed her eyes, and said again, "It sure is."

You Too?

Moments before Jesus ascended into heaven, He asked something of those who followed close behind Him — to make disciples and baptize them.

> "All authority in heaven and on earth has been given to me. Therefore go and make disciples of all nations, baptizing them in the name of the Father and of the Son and of the Holy Spirit, and teaching them to obey everything I have commanded you.

And surely I am with you always, to the very end
of the age."

MATTHEW 28:18–20

He didn't leave a lot of instruction beyond that, so
the question of how best to do it has been, and likely
always will be, up for debate. With the rise of social
media and the interconnectedness of our millennial
generation, what's the best way to fulfill the Great
Commission? With so many on the margins of Christianity, shoved out as a result of their theological leanings, sexual orientation, political beliefs, and more, do
the traditional formulas of discipleship and evangelism
still work?

I contend that we're in the middle of a significant shift, and the ways we approach both Christians
and non-Christians alike should change to reflect the
desires of the generation—desires such as significance,
relationship, a sense of purpose, and connection with
others.

We're spending tons of money, reading a ton of
books, and downloading endless podcasts trying to figure out the best way to evangelize and make disciples.
Rick McKinley, the pastor of the church we attended in
Portland, wrote a brilliant book titled *A Kingdom Called
Desire*. His entire first chapter addresses Christianity's
obsession with "how." When talking about the question
of "how," he says we're addicted to it. We buy how-to
books and look for all the best-laid plans, but in the end,

they fail us. But then another how-to idea comes along, promising that it will *fix all the things!* But it fails too.

By constantly asking "how," Rick thinks we're asking the wrong question, and I think he's right. Rather than asking "how," what if we asked "who" or "why" or both? If we change the question to ask *who* we would reach out to, our minds immediately go to the people we have relationships with, and I don't think that's a coincidence. If we changed the question to ask *why* we evangelize at all, we would likely answer with the Scripture that cites the Great Commission, and then we'd declare that it's about loving someone enough to share the gospel with them.

I think a lot of the cynicism and skepticism found in the millennial generation has, in some way, been shaped and forged in the fires of the "how" question. Because out of the "how" question, programs are born rather than relationships. And if there's one thing we're sick of, it's programs. Much good has been done by those who focus on the "how" questions, and we'd be smart to remember that. But the desires of people, specifically the millennial generation, aren't for another well-designed program. We desire something deeper, truer, and more lasting.

Storytelling and personal narrative have the ability to reach the elusive millennial generation, the ones shoved out, marginalized, and made to feel "other" or "less than." When you're the one on the fringes, one of the most powerful things someone can say to you is, "Me too." And really, it's one of the most powerful things someone can say to *anyone*, regardless of status or social placement. The intrinsic value of mutual understanding and experience is immeasurable and priceless. Mutual understanding and sharing one's experience are really just other ways to say "relationship." Relationships are priceless, and relationships are built on stories shared.

One of my favorite quotes is from author C. S. Lewis: "Friendship ... is born at that moment when one man says to another: 'What! You too? I thought that no one but myself ...'"[13] And you don't get to that moment of "You too?" without being vulnerable and sharing a bit of yourself with someone else.

That's how we get to know each other—we tell each other our struggles and victories. We talk about our pasts and how those pasts have shaped us and changed us into who we are today. We talk about the experiences in our lives that affect us, and we talk about the ways other people throughout our lives have changed us too.

We speak.

These shared stories and this retelling of ourselves are the things that build relationships. A relationship deepens when the stories get longer and more intricate, and a relationship deepens when the number of stories shared between people grows. The more we are open, honest, and true with each other, the more wholehearted and meaningful our friendships and relationships are.

I'll admit it takes me a while to build enough trust

with someone to really share the darkest and most intimate parts of my life story. But I've learned that as I trust someone with more and more pieces of my life along the way, my friendship with that person becomes stronger and more intense and intimate. It's a beautiful by-product of choosing to be vulnerable and honest with another person.

With relationship comes trust and faith between friends. This is the missing piece of the evangelism puzzle that we've been looking for. Most of us who grew up in or around church and Christian culture have been told that the cross of Jesus is a salvation bridge between us and God. Some of us have handed out our tracts and cold-called strangers on the street to tell them about the glorious salvation of Jesus Christ.

But really, it's a lot simpler than that. Evangelism should simply be another by-product of genuine relationship with others. When we build relationships with others through the sharing of stories, we earn each other's trust. When trust and faith in each other is built, we're able to ask deeper, more sincere questions about harder topics like religion. And when we talk about the harder topics with a strong foundation of friendship, there's a level of understanding that ensures the conversation will be built on love.

Instead of coming up with diagrams and well-laid plans to reach the lost, what if we just did what we normally do — make friends with people? It lasts longer and is stronger and more honest. It's without agenda.

It may be simple, but it's not easy. It actually involves greater risk — risk of being hurt or betrayed. But it's deeper, truer, and long-term. As Laurie said, there's nothing more dangerous than love, but it's also the greatest commandment Jesus gave:

> "'Love the Lord your God with all your heart and with all your soul and with all your mind.' This is the first and greatest commandment. And the second is like it: 'Love your neighbor as yourself.' All the Law and the Prophets hang on these two commandments."
>
> MATTHEW 22:37 – 40

Maybe we just need to start loving our neighbor.

Make a friend.

Tell them a story.

Listen to theirs.

I AM DAMAGED GOODS

Sarah Bessey

I was nineteen years old and crazy in love with Jesus when that preacher told an auditorium I was "damaged goods" because of my sexual past. He was making every effort to encourage this crowd of young adults to "stay pure for marriage." He was passionate, yes, well-intentioned, and he was a good speaker, very convincing indeed.

And he stood up there and shamed me, over and over and over again.

Oh, he didn't call me up to the front and name me. But he stood up there and talked about me with such *disgust*, like I couldn't be in that real-life crowd of young people worshiping in that church. I felt spotlighted and singled out among the holy   surely my red face announced my guilt to everyone.

He passed around a cup of water and asked us all to spit into it. Some boys horked and honked their worst into that cup while everyone laughed. Then he held up that cup of cloudy saliva from the crowd and asked, "Who wants to drink this?!"

And everyone in the crowd made barfing noises. *No way, gross!*

"This is what you are like if you have sex before marriage," he said seriously. "You are asking your future husband or wife to drink this cup."

Over the years the messages melded together into the common refrain: "Sarah, your virginity was a gift and you gave it away. You threw away your virtue for a moment of pleasure. You have twisted God's ideal of sex and love and marriage. You will never be free of your former partners; the boys of your past will haunt your marriage like soul ties. Your virginity belonged to your future husband. You stole from him. If — *if!* —you ever get married, you'll have tremendous baggage to overcome in your marriage. You've ruined everything. No one honorable or godly wants to marry you. You are damaged goods, Sarah."

If true love waits, I heard, then I had been disqualified from true love.

In the face of our sexually dysfunctional culture, the church longs to stand as an outpost of God's ways of love and marriage, purity and wholeness.

And yet we twist that until **we treat someone like me** —and, according to this research, **80 percent of you are like me — as if our value and worth were tied up in our virginity.**

We, the majority nonvirgins in the myopic purity conversations, feel like the dirty little secret, the not-as-goods, the easily judged example. In this clouded swirl of shame, our sexual choices are the barometer of our righteousness and worth. We can't let anyone know, so we keep it quiet, lest anyone discover we were not virgins on some mythic wedding night. We don't want to be the object of disgust or pity or gossip or judgment.

And in the silence, our shame—and the lies of the enemy—grows.

And so here, now, I'll stand up and say it, the way I wish someone had said it to me fifteen years ago when I was sitting in that packed auditorium with my heart racing, wrists aching, eyes stinging, drowning and silenced by the imposition of shame masquerading as ashes of repentance:

So, you had sex before you were married.

It's okay.

Really. It's okay.

There is no shame in Christ's love. Let him without sin cast the first stone. You are more than your virginity—or lack thereof—and more than your sexual past.

Your marriage is not doomed because you said yes to the boys you loved as a young woman. Your husband won't hold it against you; he's not that weak and ego-driven. Choose a man marked by grace.

It's likely you would make different choices, if you knew then what you know now, but, darling, don't make it more than it is, and don't make it less than it is. Let it be true, and don't let anyone silence you or the redeeming work of Christ in your life out of shame.

Now, in Christ, you're clear, like Canadian mountain water, rushing and alive, quenching and bracing, in your wholeness.

Virginity isn't a guarantee of healthy sexuality or

marriage. **You don't have to consign your sexuality to the box marked "Wrong."** Your very normal and healthy desires aren't a switch to be flipped. Morality tales and false identities aren't the stuff of a real marriage. Purity isn't judged by outward appearances and technicalities. The sheep and the goats are not divided on the basis of their virginity. (Besides, this focus is weird and over-realized; it's the flip side of the culture's coin, which values women only for their sexuality. It's also damaging not only for you but for the virgins in the room too. Really, there's a lot of baggage from this whole purity movement heading out into the world.)

For I am convinced, right along with the apostle Paul, that "neither death nor life, neither angels nor demons, neither the present nor the future, nor any powers, neither height nor depth, nor anything else in all creation, will be able to separate us from the love of God that is in Christ Jesus our Lord" (Romans 8:38–39). Not even "neither virginity nor promiscuity" and all points between can separate you from this love. You are loved—without condition—beyond your wildest dreams already.

I would say: "Sarah, your worth isn't determined by your virginity. What a lie."

No matter what that preacher said that day, no matter how many purity balls are thrown with sparkling upper-middle-class extravagance, no matter the purity rings and the purity pledges, no matter the judgmental, gospel-negating rhetoric used with the best of intentions, no matter the "how close is too close?"

serious conversations of boundary-marking young Christians, no matter the circumstances of your story, **you are not disqualified** from life or from joy or from marriage or from your calling or from a healthy and wonderful lifetime of sex because you had — and, heaven forbid, *enjoyed* — sex before you were married.

Darling, young one burning with shame and hiding in the silence, listen now: Don't believe that lie. You never were, you never will be, damaged goods.[14]

RESPONSES

Thank you, Sarah, for writing this blog. I've dealt with so much emotional baggage and pain for four years and needed to read this.

Rachel

Sarah, this post was an amazing read for me and spoke to me in words no one's ever said to me before.

Sarah

I never quite let myself realize it before now, how I have felt this shame all this time. Slowly, grace has percolated a trust in me ... And these words He's led you to write are one step closer. I appreciate how this truth has taken hold of my heart, looked me in the eye, and inspired me to choose it.

Amy

Thank you. Thank you. I am in tears reading this from the grace that you are showing me. And this line: "It's likely you would make different choices, if you knew then what you know now, but, darling, don't make it more than it is, and don't make it less than it is."

Oh, how my heart needed to read this. In regard to my having sex before marriage and to choices I made with the consequences of having sex. My heart still aches. But grace entered this morning, and my heart is a little less fragile.

Thank you.

Brittany

Sarah, I can't tell you how I needed to hear this. Redemption. Grace. Love. Humility.

I've had those things from God and from my husband, but never from the church. Never from another believer.

THANK YOU.

BA

> The kingdom is blessed —
> people are freed and healed
> and transformed —
> when we have the courage to tell.

PART 3

The Outcome:

Story Changes the World

Story Can Proclaim God at Work in Our Cities

What you do in the present — by painting, preaching, singing, sewing, praying, teaching, building hospitals, digging wells, campaigning for justice, writing poems, caring for the needy, loving your neighbor as yourself — will last into God's future. These activities are not simply ways of making the present life a little less beastly, a little more bearable, until the day when we leave it behind altogether . . . They are part of what we may call building for God's kingdom.

N. T. WRIGHT, *SURPRISED BY HOPE*

Most of my friends are evangelical Christians. My work of managing a Christian website with a bunch of Christian authors also puts me in contact with a lot of Christians. And the number one thing I'm asked when I tell people I live in Salt Lake City, whether it's in phone conversations with friends who live in another part of the country or at conferences, is this: "What's it like in Utah? Is it as Mormon as people make it out to be?"

The question is usually accompanied by some sense of disbelief that Erik and I chose to move here of our own free will. We didn't *have* to move here for a job or any sort of other obligation. We simply wanted to. In addition to our church plant, we're outdoor junkies, and for our kind there's no better place to live than Utah. There's also the emerging food scene, the live music, the beautiful weather, the Sundance Film Festival, the amazing farmers market, and world-class skiing. Not only did we want to move here for the overall level of awesome that happens in this city, but we had dear friends here who also made the move to be a part of the new church community in the downtown area of Salt Lake City.

Since most of my friends are of the evangelical Christian variety, we all speak a similar language, and we function according to the norms of our culture. One of those norms is a suspicion of the Church of Jesus Christ of Latter-day Saints (LDS), otherwise known as the Mormon Church. Sometimes calling the LDS Church "apostate" or "heretical," we can have strong words for the Mormons and their prophet, Joseph Smith. I have my own theories about where all of the hate comes from, but I won't go into that here.

Many of the friends who visit, and even local Christians, comment on how Salt Lake City is "such a dark place." In Christianese, that means there aren't a lot of other Christians among the many Mormons in Salt Lake City. I usually shrug my shoulders and offer a sarcastic remark. I don't really see it as dark. It's a lot brighter than our previous home in Portland, but I'll admit that it just might be the sunshine talking.

God in Salt Lake City

Salt Lake City is unlike any other city in the United States, really. An entire city was founded on a counter-cultural belief system, and today it is still considered one of, if not the most, religious cities in the country, in the second-most religious state in the union (only behind Mississippi).[15] When you talk about "The Church" in SLC, you're talking about the LDS Church, not the body of Christ that believers in other cities would refer to. The scope of the LDS's influence is unmatched in this city. It's nearly impossible to get elected to public office without being Mormon. They have influence over TV stations, radio stations, shopping malls, private businesses, public policy, city planning and legislation, and more.

One night, when Erik and Rowan had gone swimming at a local community center, I sat on the couch with a bowl of soup for dinner, curled under our down blanket, watching the local news coverage. It was tuned to the LDS Church-owned station, though I didn't realize it at first. One of the lead stories was about new dress code restrictions for young women at Brigham Young University, a private LDS university, and how skinny jeans were beginning to be considered "immodest dress" and would no longer be allowed. I cocked my head to the side, wondering why in the world this was a newsworthy story. But then I identified the source and also the audience, which was overwhelmingly Mormon. Realizing this, I chuckled a little bit as I ate another spoonful of soup.

Because there's a long-standing belief that this city is fertile soil for conversion, most Christians get a rude awakening upon arrival. Countless church plants have come to Salt Lake City to "save the Mormons" over the last ten years, only to get burned out because they're spinning their wheels with no traction. When Christians come to Utah to "finally bring God and the gospel to Salt Lake City," a possible interpretation is that God wasn't really doing much before they arrived.

Little did they know that God's been doing incredible things in this city. Nobody brought Him here. God's been moving in and among the people for years, and it turns out that SLC isn't as "dark" as some would make it out to be.

The confusion is understandable. If you're looking for darkness, if you're *in* the darkness, you start to forget what light actually looks and feels like. The smallest change in perspective can prove to be the best way to recognize the light.

I recognize light in the stories from my friends Nate and Alexis, who work on staff with a campus ministry at the University of Utah. College students, who for so long have subscribed to false or skewed versions of God, come to know Jesus for the first time and gain new hope and understanding of a God who loves them infinitely. Or they tell me about a group of the university's baseball players, who come to church together. These guys tell their teammates about Jesus, showing to each other love and compassion and care, even in the midst of a demanding competitive sports season.

I see light in the story of a young Christian couple in our church who live next door to a single mom. I see it in the ways they help her with child care and house repairs on a weekly basis. I love hearing how they pick up her young son from the bus stop when she's at work and how they hold his hand while they walk him back to their house, offering him a seat at their kitchen table to work on his homework until Mom gets home.

I notice light in stories about families that open up their homes to young men, and sometimes whole families, who have fled the abusive and oppressive environment of the polygamist compounds in the southern part of the state. I love hearing how these families take in these hurt and scared boys, offering them a loving home with food, support, and care as they get back on their feet in a new place. Light shines as some of these families end up adopting the young boys into their own families.

The Kingdom, Here and Now

Perhaps we miss it — the kingdom. Could it be that it's breaking through the cracks in our cities' pavements and walkways and we haven't even noticed? Perhaps we don't understand what the kingdom of God really is. What is it supposed to look like? Before we attempt to proclaim God's kingdom on earth, I think it's important that we recognize and understand what the kingdom really is.

Eugene Peterson paraphrases Jesus' words in Mark like this:

Then Jesus said, "God's kingdom is like seed thrown on a field by a man who then goes to bed and forgets about it. The seed sprouts and grows —he has no idea how it happens. The earth does it all without his help: first a green stem of grass, then a bud, then the ripened grain. When the grain is fully formed, he reaps—harvest time!

How can we picture God's kingdom? What kind of story can we use? It's like a pine nut. When it lands on the ground it is quite small as seeds go, yet once it is planted it grows into a huge pine tree with thick branches. Eagles nest in it."

MARK 4:29 – 32 MSG

The kingdom of God is a subversive movement. It's in and among us, breaking through in small and big ways. Because God has always been here and been among the people, His kingdom has been here too. Where God presents Himself, His kingdom is sure to follow.

The kingdom becomes visible when we buy a meal for someone who can't afford it.

It breaks through when one more child is taken out of foster care and put into a permanent, loving home.

It's visible when babies are born and their first cries are heard throughout the hospital hallways.

The kingdom breaks through when we break bread with the LDS missionaries who come to the door.

The kingdom breaks through when we find a new way to take care of the earth.

The kingdom is visible when the sick are healed and those around them lift their hands and praise God.

It also breaks through when the sick leave this life and venture into the next and those around them lift their hands and praise God all the same.

The kingdom breaks through when forgiveness is given generously, when grace is the language of the day, and when those in bondage — whether of their own making or at the hand of someone else — are freed.

The kingdom is strong and unwavering; it's the foundation; it's a new reality. God, through the people who claim Him as Lord and set out to follow Him, is perfecting this earth, this place we call home. He's slowly, carefully, tenderly making it new. Some people pray for revival, for God's kingdom to be revealed. The truth is, I think revival is already happening.

Perhaps we just haven't been paying attention.

Believing that the kingdom of God is already present and breaking through on the earth presents us with an invitation, a calling as believers to partner with God in what He is accomplishing in our cities and towns around the world. We're invited to be a reflection of God's unending love for His people. We, the church, have been asked to proclaim the coming kingdom.

In this announcement, we are a part of a magnificent story — the story of God redeeming the world. We know this to be true because we've seen it in our own lives. God isn't just a character in our stories; He's the one who's shaping them, writing them chapter by chapter, line by line.

Rick, my former pastor in Portland, has taught me much about the kingdom — in his sermons, in staff meetings, and just in everyday conversation. He believes in the power of the kingdom to change the world for good. He believes God is glorified immensely when we partner with Him to blow open the doors and let Him roll in. Rick wanted to do just that, and he believed that our church — our community and the people in it — could make it happen.

So he reached out to the city — the mayor's office, to be exact, as well as members of the city council — and asked them what they needed. That was it. Just a simple conversation. A pastor approaching a city official to ask, "What's your greatest need? How can we help?" was the last thing Sam Adams, the mayor of Portland at the time, was expecting.

Portland, as I mentioned earlier, is a passionately secular city. It's liberal, antiestablishment, open to "spirituality" but not overly friendly to organized religion. The church in Portland had always done its thing on its own, and the city sort of tolerated it. So to have a pastor of a large congregation come knocking and asking to talk was, well, unexpected, to say the least.

After a few conversations Rick had with Mayor Adams, Kevin Palau, and a few other church leaders in the city, it became clear that the city's schools were hurting and in dire need. So the mayor and his office asked the churches of Portland if they would use their time and resources to love the schools of Portland. It made sense that this was an important project, and it made sense for us to respond positively.

If you think about it, schools are in some ways at the center of communities in cities. It's where every day we send our most beloved — our children — to learn, grow, and mature. It's where kids make friends; it's where imaginations are nurtured; it's where societies are built. This all happens inside the walls of our schools. Ideally, we build relationships with teachers, and the teachers get to know us and our children. Sometimes they even become privy to the goings-on of our home lives and the struggles of our everyday. So by nurturing these relationships and coming alongside neighborhood schools, we were serving the children and families of some of the neediest neighborhoods in the city.

The poorest people of Portland no longer live in the immediate downtown area. They've been pushed out to the far southeast reaches of the city, saturated with crime and homelessness and broken families, often with parents in jail. The schools in southeast Portland are so neglected that the school district wanted to close down one of the high schools completely. So when the mayor asked us to step in, our church did.

We stepped up, agreeing that God is present in the city of Portland, and we committed to partnering with Him to bring about His kingdom by engaging the schools and helping families and children. We helped the poorest neighborhoods through partnering with the elementary, middle, and high schools through beautification projects, repairs and cleaning, tutoring and mentoring.

The initiative is called *Love Portland*. I was lucky enough to participate in *Love Portland* for three years before we moved to Salt Lake City. I loved noticing the smiles and looks of amazement on faces of teachers and administrators as all these people who just loved Jesus descended on their school and got to work.

One year, I pulled weeds out of concrete, laid new mulch in garden beds, and built a retaining wall. Another year, I spent hours in an elementary school library, wiping down books with Clorox wipes, organizing and filing the boxes of donated books, and cleaning off shelves. And my last year, I painted a hallway and a girls' bathroom, and I cleaned fourteen toilets alongside a team of teachers. All the while, I kept getting told, "I can't believe you all are here. I can't believe how much help you've brought."

I remember reaching over with my rubber-gloved hand and grabbing the rubber-gloved hand of the teacher next to me, looking into her eyes as they welled up with tears and telling her, "It's my pleasure. I'm so happy to help."

Rick would tell us that if we allow ourselves to be changed by the gospel, if we allow the death and resurrection of Jesus to be true in our lives, then we need to tell that story. And that story will be told through how we love our neighbors. So as an outpouring of the story of God in our own lives, we partnered with the city and loved its schools and neighborhoods. It was a beautiful picture.

It was the kingdom.

JESUS HAD BLUE EYES
(OR, "PLUS ONE")

Erika Morrison

It came one day out of the hunger in our bellies, an idea
—a way for us to weave gladness and love and other
fruit-like things into the spiritual fabric of our city. We
thought it might be a small idea, something just for
our family to do, but who knows? Maybe it can be big
and weave bright things into spiritual fabric all over the
cities of the earth.

We were having morning meditation, my three young
boys and I. It's how we start life with each new sunrise,
and this particular day there was a burning in the Spirit
and all of us were on our feet, crying and praying big ole
charismatic-y prayers against the gray walls of our living
room—though I doubt that what we prayed was bound
by our physical parameters. And when our lips buttoned
up after the heaven-bent supplications, we realized that
something had happened behind the veil, and the four
of us circled together with a thirsty urgency to respond
somehow, some way to what God was doing inside
our skin. The focus felt clearly like we were supposed
to solicit an outward movement, so I asked my guys,
"What is one more thing we can do as a family that can
help ease the suffering of this city we live in?"

(And suffer this city does, especially where we make
our home on the rim between the educated, prestigious
world of Yale University and the poorest of New Haven's
population climate. "Semi-ghetto" is what we've often

called our neighborhood because we consistently come face-to broken-face with weirdos and misfits and what some might call the "bottom dwellers" of the human race, not to mention the added edge of crime. The need and despair press hard and boldly challenge our faith to round after round of Olympic-sized stare downs.)

And do you know what they wanted to do? They decided that every time we went to the grocery store, we should make a one-bag collection of good and fun food items to drop off to a homeless person, "to show them that they're special."

Just a small idea, one more bag of groceries each time we shopped for our own bounty. Easy enough, I suppose, and it didn't seem like a time for my mama-brain to analyze the sustainability or practicality of what their little hearts wanted to give; it was just a time to respond to a moment and be present for their desire to donate from the overflow of our gifts and see if multiplication-by-sharing is, in fact, threaded through the laws of the universe like the gospel story of loaves and fishes suggests.

So we did. We went to the Elm City Market on a Tuesday, and the boys pushed their own cart alongside mine and filled a bag with love-picked edibles to give away. On our way home we drove the few extra blocks to the center green and prayed for a person who might need to feel noticed or special that day, and no sooner had the prayers left our mouths than we saw her, a homeless woman sitting on a park bench with her whole life stuffed in the big, dirty bag between her legs.

"That's her," I whispered, and we eased up to the curb, got out, and came up alongside her shoulder, looked in her eyes, and asked if she could use some groceries.

She had a bandaged wrist, and she smelled as bad as my own sin, but her tears were quick and her gratitude profuse, and we walked back to the car, slid in, and drove away with the convinced sensation that we had just fed Jesus. And it made me think about how vulnerable He must feel sometimes. When He comes to us in the hungry man, puts His heart at our mercy and wonders if we're going to feed Him — knowing that we can always turn Him down ... or nail Him up.

But it gets a little bit crazier before the day is done ...

Later that same afternoon, I dropped the boys off at their downtown art classes and asked myself what I should do with the window of kid-less space, and of course my taste buds made the decision for me, and Froyo World (frozen yogurt buffet, with abounding flavors and toppings) was where I would go. Immediately following that decision — and sure as the sun was shining that day — the next thing to slide across my conscience was simply this: "Take someone with you."

I didn't speculate very long at how this was going to happen, but quietly said "Okay" and took the few minutes during the car ride to pray the same prayer from earlier, that if there was someone who needed to feel noticed or special or just might like some ice cream and couldn't afford it, that I would know who that person was.

With the petition still warm on my lips I parallel parked, got out, and started down the sidewalk to my treat destination. A block or so before the entrance, I lifted my eyes to the distance and saw an old bum shuffling his aged feet along the concrete toward me, and the next few moments seemed to happen in slow motion as my spirit immediately touched a Reality larger than my own ... a silent murmur within echoed these words: "Oh my goodness, that's him." And my belly started flipping with anticipation, a small dose of nervousness and lastly with some seriously accelerated excitement, because you know what? Our paths collided *right in front of the door to Froyo World* (**at. the. *exact.* same. time.**), and before he could move past, I made an invitation with a bright, beaming smile stretched across my face: "I'm going to have some ice cream. Can I get you some?" And this destitute-dressed shadow-man with the long, yellowed-white beard and a few rotten teeth   he lit up like the sun had exploded inside his head.

"Well *sure*!!!" he exclaimed, and together we walked in and he piled frozen yogurt as high as his container could bear and heaped up mountains of fruit and candy.

While I was paying, this beautiful, bedraggled old man turned his blue eyes to search my brown eyes fully and asked, "Would you like to sit and eat with me?"

And right there in the middle of Froyo World, with a few dozen college students intensely watching our exchange and the cars and pedestrians making their paces outside and the employee standing behind the counter (waiting, it seemed, for my answer just as much as the homeless man was), I wanted to fall on my face and weep my shattered heart out. Because I knew that I knew that I knew that Jesus was asking me to eat ice cream with Him, and what I said past the tears clogged in my own throat were the same words this old guy had just said to me a few minutes before. "Well *sure*!!!"

Sitting outside The Yale Center for British Art, we savored our dessert, companionship, and shared stories. "Joe" was his name, and he told me some whoppers and made me laugh, and near the end he asked how old my husband was. I said "thirty-six," and with a twinkle in his voice he replied, "Oh, make sure you don't tell him about our date!" I gave my Joe a conspiratorial wink and promised it would be "our secret."

(I know what you've heard about Jesus: that He was Jewish, that naturally He had dark eyes and dark skin and a sturdy nose. But I saw Jesus that day, and He had blue eyes; sixty-five-year-old, wrinkle-lined features; and a few crumbled teeth, and we ate ice cream together.)

Do you see? We encountered the homeless Jesus on a park bench and the homeless Jesus at Froyo World, and we fed Him. And from those two Tuesday stories an idea was born, and we're calling it "Plus One." As a family we've decided we're adopting a revolving member into our tribe. Because for the last six weeks, every time we've gone food shopping at Elm City Market or bought ice cream at Froyo World or a sandwich at Green Well or dinner at The Noodle House or coffee at Starbucks, we've always bought one more to give away. And this doesn't take the place of soup kitchens or food pantries,

but comes alongside and offers something they can't
—an individual, special experience for one person.
An opportunity for one man or woman to be *seen* and
feel noticed outside the mass of their obvious brand as
"homeless."

We might be the only family that ever does "Plus One,"
and that would be fine and meaningful to me. But still,
what if—*what if* all of us, all over the country, maybe
beyond—adopted a revolving face into our heart and
fed that face every time we went out to feed ourselves?
It's just one bag or one meal or one treat at a time. But
I have heard this Bible story about how a very small
amount of food was shared, and how through that
sharing, multiplication magic happened and thousands
of hungry people were nourished.

"Plus One." It's the simplest idea, easy to remember.
Though, not once has it been *convenient* (I gave up
convenience to be a Christian). But even so, every Plus
One adventure I've participated in has been worth the
trouble because I've communed more intimately with
the person of Christ than I ever have—touching His
flesh and seeking His eyes, breaking His bread.

How it actually works, I'm sure, would vary from city to
city and person to person, because the Spirit is a lot of
things, but generic isn't one of them. And maybe you
would like to adopt someone too?[16]

RESPONSES

Oh Erika, sweet tears today reading this. I kept thinking—she is so brave, and I am so fearful. But what should we fear when He is our guide? Praying for ears to hear Him. Thank you.

Georgi

I'm so moved! I will be sharing this with my family and my small group at church in Austin, Texas.

Danielle

Beautiful. I pray for an open heart to hear God's whispers to me.

Chris

I'm in the Plus One Club effective immediately! I've been keeping filled grocery bags in the backseat of my car for the needy, but never have I broken bread with them. I'm so excited to meet Jesus again tomorrow!

Martha

Am sharing and doing.

Laura

I am so blessed by this. It has been something I have been slowly weaving into my life and this was the kick start I needed to make it a full-blown everyday practice.

Jessica

Plus One will be a part of my life, and my children will see me do it. I hope and suspect they will want to join in as well.

Shareen

Story opens our eyes
to the ways God is at work —
sometimes through us! —
in our cities.

CHAPTER 7

Story Can Advocate for Justice

We are not to simply bandage the wounds
of victims beneath the wheels of injustice;
we are to drive a spoke into the wheel itself.

DIETRICH BONHOEFFER

Here is my servant whom I have chosen,
    the one I love, in whom I delight,
I will put my Spirit on him,
    and he will proclaim justice to the nations.

MATTHEW 12:18

I'll never forget watching the movie *Taken* for the first time, settling in with some popcorn and drinks. I had heard a few of my friends talk about this movie and how intense it was, but I was not prepared for it.

The main character, played by Liam Neeson, is a retired CIA operative named Bryan Mills, who has a teenage daughter named Kim. Having seen the worst of the world during his long tenure with the CIA, Bryan is resolute in his decision to not let Kim travel to Paris with her friend, Amanda. Although Kim insists she'll be with Amanda's family the whole time, seeing the sights and museums in the city, the girls are actually going to Paris alone to follow U2 on their European tour. Unfortunately, Bryan doesn't discover this until after he gave his permission and it was too late to stop her from going.

When Kim and Amanda are kidnapped in Paris and placed in a sex trafficking ring, Bryan goes on a mission to save them. It's actually a Hollywood adaptation of a true story. So much of what you see on screen, while sensationalized, is actually rooted in a dark, appalling reality for too many women and girls around the world.

I couldn't sleep the night I watched *Taken*, and I swore to myself that my children would never travel abroad alone. Never. Ever. Watching the movie was my first real foray into the issue of human trafficking. In retrospect, it's safe to say that the dramatized, Hollywood version of trafficking was actually easier to watch than the real thing. After I got over my initial shock that sex trafficking happens to actual people, I dug into the issue.

I learned that human trafficking in the United States generates $9.5 billion in revenue every year—$32 billion globally. Approximately three hundred thousand children are at risk of being prostituted in the US alone. There are nearly two million children currently trapped in the global sex trade, and approximately 80 percent of trafficking victims are women and girls.[17] The statistics are staggering, and when you look at this picture, you wonder how it's possible to fix or even make a dent in such a monumental problem, a horrific injustice of the worst kind.

I believe God's heart breaks over injustice and that Scripture instructs us to fight against it. But how? How can you fight a $32 billion industry committing covert and perverted crimes? How can only one person make any sort of difference?

And what does "justice" really look like?

To understand what injustice looks like and how to fight it, we need to have a comprehensive understanding of what justice is. According to Tim Keller, two main words are used in Scripture to describe justice.[18] They're the Hebrew words *mishpat* and *tzadeqah*. The Hebrew word *mishpat* means the kind of justice that's given, like the rule of law, consequences for actions, or punishment for wrongdoing. The Hebrew word *tzadeqah* refers to the kind of day-to-day living in which a person conducts all their relationships, in family and society, with fairness, generosity, and equity.

If justice is more than just administering the rule of law, if we actually establish justice in the world by being generous to others and living in right relationships with those around us, then being vulnerable with our own stories has immense power in combating the evils of the world.

I was sitting in a church pew when Dr. John Perkins emerged on stage and sat down in an overstuffed armchair. It was the first time I'd heard him speak, and he'd come to talk about the relationship between justice and reconciliation and the gospel of Jesus Christ. I didn't know much about him at the time, but I'd had a few friends who really wanted to hear him.

When the crowd quieted down, the pastor conducting the interview thanked Dr. Perkins for agreeing to have this conversation in front of an audience. Dr. Perkins shared how excited he was to be there and took a sip of water. The pastor then asked him to explain a bit of his history, how he became so involved in the culture of reconciliation and justice.

As he spoke, I learned that John Perkins was born into poverty in Mississippi as a sharecropper's son in 1930. He grew up during a time of bitter racism and hatred between blacks and whites. At the age of seventeen, John's brother was murdered at the hands of a town marshal during a race-related conflict. After the urging of many around him, John fled the town and promised he would never return. Years later, in Southern California in 1960, he came to Christian faith after attending a church at the urging of his son. After hearing and believing the story of Jesus Christ, he and his wife, Vera Mae, moved back to Mississippi to share the gospel and work toward equality and reconciliation in the very hometown where his journey began.

He has been beaten, imprisoned, and harassed for his work in civil rights, with his most recent arrest in 2005 during a protest in Washington, DC — he was protesting against the government's defunding programs that benefit the poor and vulnerable. He's been given more than seven honorary doctorates — despite dropping out of school after the third grade! — and he has spoken at Harvard, Stanford, and Oxford, as well as authored nine books. I'd call him a Goliath of Christian justice and reconciliation, but after hearing him speak, I think he'd probably disagree with me.

Dr. Perkins's humility was palpable, even from the

stage, especially when the pastor mentioned all his accolades. And when he spoke about himself, he did so quietly, with reserve, and he kept his eyes fixed on the floor. When he started talking about Jesus and the gospel and redemption, though, it was like someone flipped a switch and turned him on. He became animated, almost jumping out of his chair. His voice boomed with conviction and passion. He was pointing and looking into the audience and smiling from ear to ear. There was no mistaking what mattered most to him. It was extraordinary. *He* was extraordinary, and I quickly realized what a gift it was to be listening to him.

He was asked about justice and what justice really meant in the context of living the Christian life. His answer made so much sense, yet it was so profound. He said we must begin by defining the gospel. Specifically, he said the gospel is *good news*, and because Christ atoned for our sins, we are, by grace through faith, *all* saved. That because of that atonement for all, we are all equal. We are all children of God, and in addition to this God-given equality, and because of it, our Constitution says we are endowed with certain unalienable rights—life, liberty, and the pursuit of happiness. So when those rights are minimized or taken from any one people group—because of racism, socioeconomic status, the practice of slavery, or anything else—*that* is *in*justice. It was a brilliant answer from a brilliant guy. The answer has stayed with me.

John Perkins's personal encounter with Jesus is the

very thing that prompted him and his wife to move back to Mississippi. And not just any town in Mississippi, but the town he was practically driven out of after the murder of his brother. The story of their ministry and commitment to establishing equality and justice for the poor is absolutely astounding.

In Dr. Perkins's story, we see that he is the perfect example of what it looks like to proactively *pursue* justice. That Hebrew word *tzadeqah* for "being just" means being generous with others and living in right relationship with those around us. After gaining a clear understanding of who God is and the equality He established through Jesus' giving his life on the cross, Dr. Perkins chose to live in right relationship with others—in the community where so much was taken from him. Since his return to Mississippi, Dr. Perkins has established ministries that address issues of injustice, such as segregated education, lack of affordable housing, and unemployment, and he has worked tirelessly toward achieving racial reconciliation.

His *story* has become a vehicle for justice.

Dr. John Perkins has literally changed the world around him. And if you ask him why he does the work he has, he'll likely tell you about the work of Jesus in his life first.

He'd tell you his story.

When U2's front man, Bono, realized more than two thousand verses in Scripture reference justice, the poor, and the marginalized, he remarked, "That's a lot of airtime."

Indeed.

With so much emphasis on justice and mercy throughout Scripture, it's clear that these values are at the heart of the Story of God and His redemption of the world. The God of Christianity is a God who loves justice. And if we say we follow this God, if we say we believe in Him, then we also become agents of justice.

The Old Testament prophet Jeremiah identifies what it means to *know* God: "'Did not your father have food and drink? He did what was right and just, so all went well with him. He defended the cause of the poor and needy, and so all went well. *Is that not what it means to know me?*' declares the LORD" (Jeremiah 22:15 – 16, emphasis mine).

The role we hold in the Story of God is that we've been called God's children. That's what *moves* us. We have not been welcomed as God's own to simply stand on the sidelines and hope for something to change.

We *are* the change.

When Gandhi suggested we should be the change we wish to see in the world, he might have been interpreting Jesus' words in Matthew 5:14: "You are the *light* of the world" (emphasis mine). It's our job and responsibility as believers, as children of redemption, to shine the light of hope, of truth, of justice into the darkest of places.

We do that by living and sharing the Story that is good.

John Perkins understood this. His story of salvation was his motivation for pursuing justice.

So, what will that look like in our lives? How will we combat something as big as human trafficking? Or how will we fight against the forces of injustice — racism, sexism, discrimination, abuse, and more?

Like John Perkins, we will tell the story of how God so loves us. We will tell the story that changes everything.*

---

*For information on justice advocacy organizations, see the resources section in the back of this book.

LOSING MANDELA

Kelley Nikondeha

How appropriate that my South African sister broke the news to me—Mandela died.

I picked my daughter up from school, and before we were out of the carpool lane, I cried again, telling her Madiba died. "The South African president?" she asked. We read his story many times last year over dinner, so she knew it well enough to share my tears.

We drove to the store and picked out bunches of white lilies, a pillar candle, and some ice cream. "Why do we need ice cream to remember Mandela?" she asked. I told her that comfort food would be part of our mourning, so we picked up a carton of chocolate chip. Once home, we arranged the flowers and lit the candle, and my daughter brought her book out—the one with his likeness on the front cover—and propped it up on the kitchen counter as part of our makeshift vigil.

It surprised me that the checkout clerk didn't know his name. "Is he a soccer player from Africa?" Even friends of mine confessed that beyond his name, they knew nothing of the man or his story.

I was aghast. **How could people not know about Mandela —a modern luminary and practitioner of liberation?**

I encouraged my daughter to take her book to school the next day. I crossed my fingers, hoping her teacher would read the book to his class. He did. And I felt like I did some small thing to ensure one class of fourth graders would know who Nelson Mandela was and why his life mattered.

I added my own book, his *Long Walk to Freedom*, to our vigil. "Mama, when I get old enough, can I read this Mandela book?" she asked, running her long fingers across the eight hundred-plus pages. I swelled with pride. "Yes, someday you can read his words for yourself and know why he means so much to us."

Days later, I would stay up to watch Mandela's body lowered into the sun-soaked slopes of Qunu. I blew out the candle. Tossed the wilted lilies into the garbage. Put the books away. Losing Mandela marked me somehow.

As I placed the candle on the shelf of my iconostasis, still warm from days of burning, I knew it was time to move from mourning to living, embodying his legacy. For a moment I thought of those who couldn't mourn with me, because they couldn't mourn a man they never knew. It was a dull ache I took to bed with me.

* * *

But I now offer a confession of my own. There are names, voices, and stories I know nothing of. Other luminaries fighting for freedom and people living on the wrong side of justice remain invisible to me. While I cannot know each story, I can be attentive to more. **I must cast my net wider; I must lean in and listen better to those who could teach me a more excellent way.**

So I've determined this year I will do better. **I will read more memoirs; I will listen to the voices on the margins.**

I've already collected books by wise Aboriginal mothers, a Gambian man who grew into a scholar, a Lebanese journalist speaking of rebuilding his homeland, a Latina lawyer (and Supreme Court justice) from the Bronx, a Romanian Jew who survived multiple concentration camps, an American Muslim woman from my hometown, and an Iranian woman who lived through the Islamic Revolution. I hope to hear their stories with an open heart and allow their experiences to educate, challenge, and stretch me.

I plan to widen my circle online—who I follow and what articles I read. I want to be aware of those in my own neighborhood who can become teachers or point the way to new sources to expand my imagination. I don't want these people to leave without having taught me their lessons, without imparting a blessing.

Maybe in losing Mandela, I will gain many other luminaries to light my way as I continue the long walk to freedom.[19]

RESPONSES

I love how you brought this around to introspection for all of us. We can always cast our nets wider, and you've inspired me to do the same.

Sarah

I needed your words this morning. I needed to know more than a cursory glance at a faraway historical figure. We need to hear stories beyond our own reach. I live in a country where pop culture leads the "news." We know far too much about entertainers and far too little about those who are saving humanity. Thank you for bringing this to light for me. I, too, want better stories.

Jem

Oh, Kelley, what a wonderful tribute, and such an important way to respond. I will be following your journey as well, friend. This is one I am just beginning as well.

Cara

The sharing of stories is a tool in advocating for justice.

CHAPTER 8

Story Can Proclaim
God's Kingdom

God's kingdom is present in its beginnings, but still
future in its fullness. This guards us from an under-
realized eschatology (expecting no change now) and
an over-realized eschatology (expecting all change
now). In this stage, we embrace the reality that while
we're not yet what we will be, we're also no longer
what we used to be.

**TIMOTHY KELLER,
"PRINCIPLES OF KINGDOM MINISTRY"**

The kingdom of God is within you.

LEO TOLSTOY

"The kingdom of God is in your midst."

LUKE 17:21

Most days I have grand intentions of waking up before my kids do. The combination of my being a heavy sleeper and being just plain lazy, however, means it usually doesn't happen. My alarm clock is my new daughter, Scout, who is now six months old. Typically, she is up and ready to eat between five and six o'clock in the morning, which, by my standards, is pretty freaking early. With this baby who wakes up early, and an equally demanding preschooler, I'm lucky if I get a shower most days. I usually have to settle for a splash of cold water on my face and a strong cup of coffee. And by strong, I mean I like it to kick me in the teeth.

Because of four-year-old Rowan's autism spectrum disorder, we try to stick to a somewhat rigid routine so he can function well. Rowan thrives when he knows what to expect, and transitions are especially difficult for him. Among the things that happen every day, Rowan gets a cup of milk without delay upon entering the kitchen in the morning. Then he watches cartoons while he eats breakfast. This morning it's *Mickey Mouse Clubhouse*—so, once again, I'm forced to listen to the theme song for the one millionth time. Today I consider reaching through the TV screen and ripping off Mickey's ears. I'm really starting to dislike that mouse.

The rest of the day is a pretty rigid schedule of preschool drop-off, nap times, working hours for me, laundry, cleaning, preschool pick-up, grocery shopping, cooking, more nap times, more work hours, cooking again, the bedtime routine, and a partridge in a pear tree.

It's normal, everyday life. It's not glamorous. It's not extraordinary. It's what I do.

This kind of mundane routine is not celebrated in our culture. Every time we turn on a TV, flip through a magazine, or even pick up a book, we're told, over and over again, something that isn't true: the stories we are living with our lives are *not enough*.

How you've treated your body isn't good enough. You need to lose weight so you can look like the thin model in the Christian Dior advertisement, wearing clothes that nobody can afford. Speaking of money, you don't make enough, which is unfortunate because your coolness quota depends on the newness of your technology. Oh, you have an old Apple product? That's a shame. You should try this new gadget. I swear it'll change your life. The crisp clean screen makes it *so* much easier to read books. And that car you're driving? You'd be happier if you drove a Mercedes.

We swallow these lies for years, and before we know it, we're so unsatisfied with our lives that we'd do anything to change them — even at great sacrifice to our families, our relationships, and our communities. Satisfaction can even come at great sacrifice to our intimate relationship with Jesus.

Here's the reality: Some people are living the lives Hollywood movies, great novels, and stage productions are made of. Some people are living absolutely fantastical lives, to which I say, "Well done!" But the flip side is that *most* people aren't living lives full of extraordinary events and circumstances. Most people are living life by daily fulfilling the obligations set before them. To most, these lives don't seem like anything to write home about. And though you may be living what seems like an ordinary life, faithfully doing what God has placed in front of you to do means you are actually living an extraordinary story.

Simply put, we Christians live a great story when we are being faithful. And the kingdom is made visible in the mundane when we forgo what's *attractive* for what is *obedient*.

In my own life, this has looked like staying home with my kids during their early years. Before giving birth to Rowan, I was building a career. I loved my job at the church. I had no intention of giving it up when I started. But when Rowan was born, I knew my purpose had changed. I knew God was moving me into a new season of life — that I was now meant to stay home rather than go back to work after my maternity leave was over. This isn't to say I didn't make this decision kicking and screaming. I did. But in the end, I chose to be faithful to what God was calling me into.

And because of my choice to listen and respond, I was able to recognize in Rowan's development the small signals indicating that something might be off. I was able to walk through every step of his diagnosis without missing a beat. I was able to provide him with more consistent and regulated care at home so he could flourish and improve, despite his disability. I know that staying home provided a sense of comfort and regularity for my child, who can't process transitions well. Because I chose to listen, I was able to give my child what he needed in some of his hardest days in the early years — a parent at home full-time.

It looks like a normal life. It may or may not even look very much like sacrifice. But because it was a response to God's leading, it's a good story.

As I mentioned earlier in this book, *story* has become a huge buzzword in Christian culture these days. Everyone is talking about it, and everyone wants to know how to "live a good story." But I'm here to remind you of a fundamental truth: no matter how mundane, you're already living a great story that the world around you needs to hear. Not everyone is meant to start an orphanage in Ethiopia, evangelize to the poor in India, open up a microfinance nonprofit in Los Angeles, or write a book in Salt Lake City (see what I did there?).

Here's what you were meant to do: be faithful.

If that looks like finishing your lab work in your chemistry class, then be faithful and finish. If that looks like putting your kid in time-out for hitting the dog for the tenth time, then be faithful. Do it eleven times if you need to. If being faithful looks like filling out one more spreadsheet in your boring paralegal job, then be faithful and fill out that spreadsheet. These are the stories we need to begin to recognize.

As a mom of young children, I need an older mom to tell me her stories of parenting. I need to hear how she went through seasons of wanting to throw in the towel, or how she never thought she was enough, or how she was often tired beyond reason but somehow made it through another day. I need to hear those stories to encourage me to keep going, to keep pushing onward in what *I'm* called to do at this time in my life. I need the gift of perspective, spoken from a mom who's been there, to remind me to tell myself, "Yes, I can do this again today."

As a writer, I need other published authors to tell me their stories of rejection. I need to hear their stories of frustration as they painstakingly type out their manuscripts, fighting for every word and every sentence. I need to be reminded that, yes, writing is work. It's not always romantic. I need the stories of success. And I need other writers to tell me how their work has touched the lives of others. When I'm ready to give up, I need the stories to remind me that what I do is worth it.

Those stories of faithfulness change me. They motivate me. They encourage me to keep being faithful and keep plugging away at what God has given me, even when I just want to give up.

What you're doing may not be as important as the *how*. If you're being faithful in what God has called you to do, He is transforming you and molding you to be more like Christ today than you were yesterday. And that is the greatest story you could ever tell. The story of how God is transforming you is how God's kingdom breaks in on earth today.

So, what could it look like for my own story of redemption to proclaim the coming of God's kingdom in Salt Lake City? In my church community? In the everyday rhythm of my own life? I can't say I have it figured out. I'm still in the process of learning what it means to love my neighbors well, especially as a stay-at-home mom with two small children.

Though I'd love to be more active in the community, my day-to-day, which is relatively isolating, makes it difficult during this season. I'm not a part of the professional world where I enter an office and work a nine-to-five job. So I'm doing my best with the space where I am. Both *A Deeper Story* and my own blog are spaces I'm trying to steward well as the setting for my own story to be shared for others to read. I've been blessed and honored to receive emails and notes from readers telling me how my willingness to be honest about my life has changed them in some way, has brought them closer to Jesus. In my book, there's no higher compliment.

I'm trying to always leave my door open—figuratively, of course, because I have two dogs that bolt anytime they're given an inch to squeeze through. I try to make my home a welcoming place for anyone who enters it. Laurie, Michael, and others who stand, homeless and asking passersby for money, on the corner at the entrance to the grocery store across the street, know they can always knock on my door.

I live next door to a group of college kids who like to party, so I've been known to walk next door with some freshly ground coffee and a bag of bagels to cure the hangovers.

On Halloween night, I make a big batch of hot apple cider to pass out to the doting and devoted parents taking their kids trick or treating.

Because we live in one of the most liberal, unchurched areas of town, we're a hot spot for the LDS missionaries who go door-to-door. They've had dinner at my kitchen table, played with my kids, and told me about their families, with whom they have minimal to no contact during their two-year mission.

When public policy and local legislative issues come up that might negatively affect my neighbors or my homeless friends, I put in a call to my state representatives and make sure they know where I stand and why. The outcome doesn't always fall in my favor, but I can put my head on the pillow at night and know that I tried.

And on the flip side, I've always wanted to go with folks in our congregation who minister to prostitutes and drug addicts on the west side of town, but with two small children, it's not usually feasible. So I try to grab a few extra supplies during each run to the grocery store to equip the ones who *are* serving in that way.

It's not much, I know. But it's something. It's what I'm able to do with the space and time I'm given. I'm learning to stretch myself even more to show the city of Salt Lake that yes, God is here. Yes, God is moving. Yes, God loves you. I'm doing my best to be a faithful and diligent follower of Christ, and that's the story I'm choosing to live. Part of my faithfulness in this season of my life is being a present and consistent mother to my two small children, being a supportive wife to a husband who works his tail off, and being a writer who proclaims God's kingdom and His unrelenting love to the world. It's not the stuff of blockbuster movies. It's enough, though, because for now, I'm being faithful to what God has called me to.

That's the story I'm living, and it's a good one.

As you take stock of the story you're living right now—whether it's filling out spreadsheets or putting on bedsheets—are you purposing to be faithful to the particular, *most likely mundane* thing God has called you to do?

Do it, and then *share* it.

Chances are there is someone in your orbit right now who's wondering if her or his story matters at all. As you share your very plain story of living out the stuff to which God has called you, they are set free to live and share their own.

And so on, and so on, and so on …

BREMMER'S LOSS
Seth Haines

Bremmer lost his youngest daughter. I knew her from my grade-school days, the cute fourth grader with the laugh like Woody Woodpecker. In her teens Ari smoked weed and smelled like teen spirit. In her twenties she fancied herself a medicine woman and claimed addiction to sexy ladies and heroin. She was a self-proclaimed American shaman. A transcendent spirit. A native daughter. A death wish over a birthday candle.

The morning before Ari left her corporeal vehicle, Bremmer was at the Wednesday morning prayer service with Father John. Father John asked Bremmer to pray for the group. "Ask that our blessed Christ would do what it takes, Brem. Ask that He would teach us undivided devotion." Bremmer balked, using a four-letter word. Father John did a double take and said, "Come again?" Bremmer said, "Respectfully, Father, I don't know what that means. You might *think* you want to love Christ wholeheartedly, but there's not one of us broke enough to really know." He leaned forward in the metal folding chair. "I'm not going to pray a lie."

Twenty-four hours later, Bremmer sat on the edge of his bed, rocking a hyperventilating wife. The body would be transported for burial, the ER doctor said. His daughter would be home by the end of the week. They'd bury her in the cemetery off Old Greenwood Road. It's where her grandparents and great-grandparents were buried. It's where Brem would be buried in twenty years or so.

It's cliché to say that fathers shouldn't have to bury their daughters. *So I won't say it.*

* * *

I ran into Bremmer about this time last year. We were at a professional education conference, and we bumped shoulders in the hall. It had been one year since his daughter's passing. He went straight for the jugular, no time to spare. "Son, tell me what you believe," he said. I knew what he meant, and every good answer I thought I had for grief evaporated. I stammered, "I don't know, Brem. I don't know." He pulled me up by my shoulders and looked into my eyes. He said, "I don't know why I'm telling you this, son, but here's what I know. I want you to listen."

He breathed deep, let go, and rubbed his forehead with his thumb and forefinger.

"I know the Pharisees, the pillars of the church who waited weeks before coming to see me after Ari died. I know the Holy Spirit. He visited me in a factory worker and his wife, a couple who shared supper, misery, and prayed the rosary with us once a week for a month. I know there's no substitution for a good priest and yeast rolls baked by the Sisters of Mercy. I know that Catholics can be mystics too. I know that Mary understands the sorrow in losing a child. I know that complete devotion requires complete devastation. I know I can pray now without lying. I know whom I know."

I saw the tongue of fire in Bremmer's eyes that day, and I want to *know* the God he knows.[20]

RESPONSES

I have been afraid for some time of what my longing to know God will actually bring to the reality of my life. I know what it's brought so far and won't the circumstances need to be even more pressing if I am to go deeper?

Erika

I too can't stop the longing ... Think I'll go write a response now on my experience ...

Julie

You've reminded us here, not only by your beautiful message, but in the way you shaped it. I'm left trembling and shaken and in awe.

Storytellers like you can change hearts.

Christina

I know the Pharisees, the pillars of the church as well ... they didn't wait weeks to visit. They never came to visit me. The situation was just way too messy.

But Jesus is all about messy.

He has never left me alone.

Picture Lady

Picture Lady, I hear a story in there. Would love to hear it (but no pressure). Sometimes the sharing of stories helps me understand the places in my life where I trend toward Pharisee. Really ... I'm guilty.

All in all, though, I'm glad you know an abiding Jesus.

Seth

Ah, thanks for even caring to ask. Yes, there is a story. I have written it—and here's the link ...

Picture Lady

God's kingdom is proclaimed
in its fullness when we tell
the truth about God
and about ourselves.

Thank You

Thank you, Jenni Burke and the team at DCJA, for shepherding this thing since its tiny inception and for caring about me, about the book, and about the potential of both. Thank you for being my champion.

This book would not be what it is without the brilliant minds and loving care of Carolyn McCready and Margot Starbuck. Thank you for pushing me, encouraging me, and pulling more out of me to make this book the best it could be. I'm forever indebted to your editing genius.

Thank you to the entire editing, marketing, and PR teams at Zondervan, particularly Dirk Buursma, Alicia Kasen, and Jennifer VerHage. And a monumental thank you to Shauna Niequist, who said yes before I could even finish my sentence. Thank you for saying, "Anything I can do to help." Thank you for your incredible talent and for sharing it here. What a gift it is to know you and to call you friend.

This book wouldn't exist without the Deeper Story

community of editors, writers, and readers. You are the reason that I believe in the power of story. Your bravery, honesty, and vulnerability have changed the hearts of countless people around the world, including mine. Thank you for everything. Thank you to Seth Haines, whose story of healing helped me love the church again. And thank you to Amber, who told me to listen to him. Thank you to Preston Yancey for the accountability, the encouragement, and the countless "you can do this" messages.

Thank you to Rogue Coffee Roasters in Grants Pass, Oregon, and The Rose Establishment in Salt Lake City for providing me with endless caffeine, sustenance, and atmosphere to get this thing written. And thank you to Explosions in the Sky, M83, Jay-Z and Kanye West, Bon Iver, Capital Cities, Ingrid Michaelson, and so many others for your musical talent that played in my headphones while writing and editing.

All my love, affection, unicorns, candles, and inappropriate thoughts to my favorite band of misfits — Jessica and Matthew Paul Turner, Kristen Howerton, Rachel Held Evans, Jamie Wright, Jason and Aimee Boyett, Justin and Rachel Shumaker, Kevin Shoop, Stephanie Drury, Adam and Dana Ellis, Alise Wright, David Henson, Ed Cyzewski, Jimmy Spencer Jr., Sharideth Smith, Tamara Lunardo, Zack Hunt, Holly Zaher, Caleb Wilde, and Matt Wilson.

To the Thinklings, the loveliest creatives I know — thank you for your support, your camaraderie, your friendship. Thank you to the fierce sisterhood who carried me all the way, who lifted my arms when I was too tired, who believed in me when I didn't believe in myself — Sarah Bessey, Laura Tremaine, Ashleigh Baker, Amber Haines, Allison Olfelt, Abby Hollingsworth, Arianne Segerman, Chris Ann Brekhus, Emily Carter, Jen Johnson, Joy Bennett, Kelly Gordon, Kelly Sauer, Kristin Potler, Leigh Kramer, Lora Lynn Fanning, Megan Cobb, Megan Tietz, and Missy Dollahon. My wise, cunning, and innocent sisters, I love you so much.

To the many people who loved and cared for my children so I could scribble out the words in this book — Kassidy Sharp, Karen Brittain, Travis and Claire Tocher, Jeanne Fields, Ellie Debo, Nicole Brown, Molly Person, and Susanna Phinney — thank you, and I'm sorry. To Jim Crystal and the entire OTT family, thank you for loving, supporting, and encouraging us, year after year.

To the people of Missio Dei Community, particularly the avenues house church — thank you for always pointing me to Jesus time and time again and for loving me, my family, and the mess of my life and house. Thank you for filling our home with so much joy and compassion week after week. I'm sorry I'm so distracted during Bronco games. Thank you to Kyle and Joy Costello, Abby Staible, Tricia Staible, and Lucas Muller for asking the hard questions, for supporting me from the beginning, and for praying. I love you.

To my parents, Glenn and Bonnie Bilawsky, and for my brothers, Nick and Ryan — thank you for nurturing me, for planting the seeds by saying, "You're such a good writer." Thank you for believing in me and always being a safe place. Thank you to Matt Weiseth, Karen Weiseth, Bruce Comstock, Ed and Ginny Weiseth, and Tommy and Amie O'Toole for always cheering me on.

To my beloved and wild children, Rowan Matthew and Scout Margot—I am so blessed to be your mother, and I am so excited to see you both write your own stories. I love you to the moon and back, and you'll always be Mommy's sunshine.

To Erik, the light and love of my life—thank you for choosing me. Thank you for nights at St. Marks, for a weekend at Suttle Lake, for dinners on the Rogue, for days at Winter Park, for mornings in bed and glasses of red at the kitchen table. Thank you for holding me when I'm scared. Thank you for pushing me when I refuse to move; thank you for pulling me closer when I try to run. Thank you for choosing to say yes at the altar, and thank you for choosing to say yes every day since. I am lost without you. Thank you for always taking me to Jesus. I'm yours.

Organizations That Are
Advocating for Justice

INTERNATIONAL JUSTICE MISSION
(ijm.org)

About

International Justice Mission (IJM) is a human rights agency that brings rescue to victims of slavery, sexual exploitation, and other forms of violent oppression. IJM lawyers, investigators, and aftercare professionals work with local officials to secure immediate victim rescue and aftercare, to prosecute perpetrators, and to ensure that public justice systems—police, courts, and laws—effectively protect the poor.

Core Commitments

In the tradition of heroic Christian leaders like abolitionist William Wilberforce and transformational leaders like Mother Teresa and Martin Luther King Jr., IJM's staff stand against violent oppression in response to the Bible's call to justice (Isaiah 1:17) — seek justice, rescue the oppressed, defend the orphan, plead for the widow.

IJM seeks to restore to victims of oppression the things that God intends for them — their lives, their liberty, their dignity, the fruits of their labor. By defending and protecting individual human rights, IJM seeks to engender hope and transformation for those it serves and restore a witness of courage in places of oppressive violence. IJM helps victims of oppression, regardless of their religion, ethnicity, or gender.

Contact
International Justice Mission
PO Box 58147
Washington, DC 20037
703-465-5495
703-465-5499 (fax)
contact@ijm.org (email)
Office hours: 9:00 a.m. to 5:30 p.m. EST

THE EXODUS ROAD
(theexodusroad.com)

About

The Exodus Road exists to empower the rescue of victims of sexual slavery. Operating primarily in Southeast Asia, we believe a major component of fighting human trafficking and child slavery lies in working with local law enforcement to find situations of trafficking and to then assist in the rescue of victims and the prosecution of criminals. By decreasing the profitability of the trafficking industry for the criminal, we will eventually slow the mechanisms that make the exploitation of women and children so lucrative.

The Exodus Road is not a single investigative organization, but rather it is a network of surveillance teams and individuals committed to fight trafficking, one legal court case at a time. Currently, we are working with fifteen operatives, representing seven different investigative organizations. Collectively, our team's past experience has played a role in the rescue of more than six hundred victims and the prosecution of nearly 350 legal cases. Most are current or former police or military men.

Core Commitments

The main focus at The Exodus Road is in connecting funds from the West with undercover surveillance and rescue operations in the East. With on-the-ground accountability in place, The Exodus Road stays connected to its operatives and learns of their needs for surveillance equipment, funds for particular operations, or investigative training, and then we take those needs to the Western community through fund-raising efforts like grant writing, public speaking, church events, and social media venues. With our network on the ground to oversee projects, we are able to channel particular grants or funds for requested needs from our field officers. Our hope is to become the fuel of finances, which will empower the noble men and women who are fighting for targeted interventions in some of the darkest places on earth.

Secondary goals of our organization are increasing awareness of the realities of human trafficking, inspiring the Western community to give generously on behalf of the modern-day slave, and facilitating connections within the local intervention and investigative community. We have a team of bloggers, artist advocates, and volunteers who sacrificially work to that end.

Contact
    The Exodus Road
    PO Box 7591
    Woodland Park, CO 80863
    202-656-6814
    info@theexodusroad.com (email)

WORLD VISION
(worldvision.org)

About

World Vision is a Christian humanitarian organization dedicated to working with children, families, and their communities worldwide to reach their full potential by tackling the causes of poverty and injustice. Working in nearly one hundred countries around the world, World Vision serves all people, regardless of religion, race, ethnicity, or gender.

Core Commitments

We are called to serve the neediest people of the earth — to relieve their suffering and to promote the transformation of their condition of life. We stand in solidarity in a common search for justice. We seek to understand the situation of the poor and work alongside them toward fullness of life. We share our discovery of eternal hope in Jesus Christ.

We seek to facilitate an engagement between the poor and the affluent that opens both to transformation. We respect the poor as active participants, not passive recipients, in this relationship. They are people from whom others may learn and receive, as well as give. The need for transformation is common to all. Together we share a quest for justice, peace, reconciliation, and healing in a broken world.

Contact
World Vision
34834 Weyerhaeuser Way South
Federal Way, WA 98001
1-888-511-6548
info@worldvision.org (email)

Notes

1. Rachel Held Evans, "Why Millennials Are Leaving the Church," http://religion.blogs.cnn.com/2013/07/27/why-millennials-are-leaving-the-church (accessed January 15, 2014).

2. Ibid.

3. Addie Zierman, "In Defense of the 4-Letter Word," http://deeperstory.com/in-defense-of-the-4-letter-word/ (accessed January 15, 2014).

4. Ashleigh Baker, "What I Won't Tell You about My Ballet Dancing Son," http://deeperstory.com/what-i-wont-tell-you-about-my-ballet-dancing-son/ (accessed January 15, 2014).

5. See? Portlanders love their beer ("Portland Brewery City Guide," www.brewhopping.com/cityguide_brewery-Portland_oR.aspx [accessed January 15, 2014]).

6. Barna Group, "Diversity of Faith in Various U.S. Cities," http://cities.barna.org/diversity-of-faith-in-various-u-s-cities/ (accessed January 15, 2014).

7. Lydia Saad, "Heavily Democratic States Are Concentrated in the East," www.gallup.com/poll/156437/Heavily-Democratic-States-Concentrated-East.aspx#2 (accessed January 15, 2014).

8. Suzannah Paul, "Walk of Shame," http://deeperstory.com/walk-of-shame/ (accessed January 21, 2014).

9. Jen Hatmaker, "For When I've Been an Earthquake ...," http://deeperstory.com/author/jen-h/ (accessed January 21, 2014).

10. Mihee Kim-Kort, "Beyond Black and White: Yellow Fever and Letting Go of Shame," http://deeperstory.com/beyond-black-and

-white-yellow-fever-and-letting-go-of-shame/ (accessed January 21, 2014).

11. Megan Tietz, "With Tingling Fingers and Shaky Voice, I Speak of Healing," http://deeperstory.com/with-tingling-fingers -and-shaky-voice-i-speak-of-healing/ (accessed January 21, 2014).

12. Beth Moore, "Sadness and Madness," http://blog.lproof.org/ 2013/04/sadness-and-madness.html (accessed January 21, 2014).

13. C. S. Lewis, *The Four Loves* (1960; repr., New York: Houghton, Mifflin, Harcourt, 1991), 78.

14. Sarah Bessey, "I Am Damaged Goods," http://deeperstory .com/i-am-damaged-goods/ (accessed January 21, 2014).This post is still our most-read post at *A Deeper Story*, and it currently has the most comments in the comment section. We still get emails, notes, and messages from readers about how this story has freed them from shame and guilt and how they are walking freely in Christ's forgiveness—all because Sarah was bold enough to share. So awesome.

15. Alex Rogers, "Where Are the Most Religious States in America in 2013?" *Time Newsfeed* (February 13, 2013), http:// newsfeed.time.com/2013/02/13/where-are-the-most-religious -states-in-america-in-2013/ (accessed January 21, 2014).

16. Erika Morrison, "Jesus Had Blue Eyes (Or, 'Plus One')," http://deeperstory.com/jesus-had-blue-eyes-or-plus-one/ (accessed January 21, 2014).

17. International Justice Mission, "Fact Sheet: Sex Trafficking," http://www.ijmuk.org/sites/default/files/documents/Sex%20 Trafficking_2.pdf (accessed January 21, 2014).

18. Tim Keller, "What Is Biblical Justice?" *Relevant* online (August 23, 2012), www.relevantmagazine.com/god/practical-faith/ what-biblical-justice (accessed January 21, 2014).

19. Kelley Nikondeha, "Losing Mandela," http://deeperstory.com/ losing-mandela/ (accessed January 21, 2014).

20. Seth Haines, "Bremmer's Loss," http://deeperstory.com/ bremmers-loss/ (accessed January 21, 2014).

A DEEPER STORY

Over 60 storytellers
Content addresses issues found
in culture, family, and the church,
using the art of storytelling.
New content every day

www.deeperstory.com

A**DEEPER**STORY

It's easy to tell someone your opinion.
It's hard work telling them your story.